"十一五"国家重点出版规划项目 　　总顾问◎ 胡壮麟　孙亦丽
全国高职高专公共英语教材　　　　总主编◎ 丁国声

新世纪
应用英语教程 1（修订版）

学生用书

苏联波　柴　明　主编

北京大学出版社
PEKING UNIVERSITY PRESS

图书在版编目(CIP)数据

新世纪应用英语教程(1)学生用书 / 苏联波,柴明主编. —2版(修订版). —北京：北京大学出版社，2009.10
(全国高职高专公共英语教材)
ISBN 978-7-301-15667-4

Ⅰ.新… Ⅱ.①苏…②柴… Ⅲ.英语–高等学校：技术学校–教学参考资料 Ⅳ.H31

中国版本图书馆 CIP 数据核字(2009)第 145593 号

书 名：	新世纪应用英语教程(1)(修订版)学生用书
著作责任者：	苏联波 柴 明 主编
策 划：	张 冰
责 任 编 辑：	刘 爽
标 准 书 号：	ISBN 978-7-301-15667-4/H·2295
出 版 发 行：	北京大学出版社
地 址：	北京市海淀区成府路 205 号　100871
网 址：	http://www.pup.cn
电 话：	邮购部 62752015　发行部 62750672　编辑部 62755217　出版部 62754962
电 子 邮 箱：	zbing@pup.pku.edu.cn
印 刷 者：	三河市北燕印装有限公司
经 销 者：	新华书店
	787毫米×1092毫米　16 开本　11.75 印张　300 千字
	2006 年 5 月第 1 版　2009 年 10 月第 2 版
	2018 年 1 月第 9 次印刷
定 价：	25.00 元(配有光盘)

未经许可，不得以任何方式复制或抄袭本书之部分或全部内容。
版权所有，侵权必究　举报电话：010-62752024
电子邮箱：fd@pup.pku.edu.cn

总顾问　胡壮麟　孙亦丽
总主编　丁国声

主　编　苏联波　柴　明
副主编　车炳银　姚　键　黎富玉　阳　勇　刘维一

编　委（以姓氏笔画顺序排名）
　　　　车炳银　刘维一　阳　勇　张春兰　李文凤
　　　　杜　洁　杨　蓓　沈　岚　苏联波　姚　键
　　　　赵建礼　柴　明　黎富玉

总 序

近年来,高等职业教育的发展规模迅速扩大,形成了"半分天下",为中国的大众化高等教育做出了重要贡献。随着规模发展,一系列的教育质量工程陆续展开。其中,规划教材和精品教材的评选均旨在提高教学水平。教改的关键是教师,教师的关键是教材,教材的关键是理念。

高职的教材建设虽然与教育快速发展现状之间的差距在缩小,但在教材建设方面仍然缺乏规划和标准,在使用和出版方面存在随意性和功利性。因此,适合高职培养目标和紧贴市场需求的高水准的教材少之又少。当务之急是认真抓好高职教材编写队伍建设,增强教材建设的精品意识,使教材的编写出版符合职业教育的规律。

高职教材可分为两大类,即文化基础课教材和专业基础课教材。北京大学出版社出版的《新世纪应用英语教程》和《新世纪交际英语教程》是一套文化基础课教材。这次修订教材的目的是使其教材定位准确、模式科学、质量上乘和内容新颖。经过编写人员的努力,新修订的教材终于焕然一新、与时俱进,反映出了高职教育的改革思路。高职教育在改革摸索,教材编写在开发探讨。希望更多的像北京大学出版社这样的权威知名机构积极关心和参与高职教育的改革和发展,使高职教育真正走上由规模发展转向质量发展的健康之路。

丁国声

全国高职高专公共英语教材　总主编

教育部高等学校高职高专英语类专业教学指导委员会　委员

修订版前言

《新世纪应用英语教程》自初版以来,得到了使用本教程各高校师生的广泛认同,认为这套教材取材丰富,题材多样,贴近生活,注重语言学习、语言实践、语言应用以及文化体验的有机结合,有利于学生语言应用能力的培养与提高。同时也提出了许多宝贵的建议和意见,为此我们对本教程进行了相应的修订,其重点如下:

一、各单元"学习指导(Guide to Text-Learning)"内容,明确单元任务,体现"任务型教学"的具体内容,培养学生自主学习的习惯。

二、个别课文做了必要的调整,以增强教材选文的时代性和趣味性。

三、增加了语法和阅读部分的练习,旨在扩大学生对所学知识的理解和应用。

四、根据外籍专家的意见对原教材中的某些语言表达进行了修改,使之更加地道。

在本教程的修订过程中,我们得到了河北外国语职业学院院长丁国声教授的悉心指导和北京大学出版社外语编辑室张冰主任的大力支持,外籍专家 Paul Stilley 和 Tiffany Nelson 不辞辛劳,对全书进行了认真的审校,在此一并表示衷心感谢。

我们希望《新世纪应用英语教程》(修订本)能更好地为高职高专学生的语言应用能力的培养与提高服务。

2009 年 7 月

前　言

　　《全国高职高专公共英语教材》是为进一步落实国家《2003—2007年教育振兴行动计划》，在广泛调研的基础上依据教育部《高等职业教育英语课程教学基本要求》(以下简称《基本要求》)特为全国高职高专非英语专业学生编写的一套公共英语教材，并被列入"十一五"国家重点出版规划项目《面向新世纪的立体化网络化英语学科建设丛书》。本套教材取材丰富，题材多样，贴近生活，时代感强，是一套集应用性、实用性、趣味性和文化性为一体的特色英语教科书。为方便学生学习和教学安排，本教材分为两大体系：《新世纪应用英语教程》(着重于读、写、译)和《新世纪交际英语教程》(着重于视、听、说)。这两大体系既相照应又相包容，不仅使听、说、读、写、译五大语言基本技能训练得到有效的整合，并科学地贯穿于英语教学的全过程，而且还从不同的角度为学生的语言学习提供生动多元的文化氛围和真实丰富的语言环境，从而使语言学习、语言实践、语言应用以及文化体验有机结合，十分有利于学生语言应用能力的培养与提高。

　　本教材为《新世纪应用英语教程》，其特色主要体现在以下几个方面：
　　1. 布局科学合理，能很好地满足《基本要求》关于分级教学、分级指导之需要。全套书共分三册，第一、二册为B级(过渡级)要求，适用于入学时英语水平较低的学生，通过学习应认知2500个英语词汇；学完第三册书达到A级(标准级)要求，应认知3400个英语词汇，词汇覆盖率达到98%；在体例编排上，通过对构成本教材主体的课文主题、语法项目、实用英语等项目的科学安排，使本教材第一、二册在相对独立而自成体系的同时与第三册形成有机联系，以方便老师的教学和学生对本教材的使用。
　　2. 针对性强，很好地体现了《基本要求》的精神。全书各项目安排均紧密围绕培养学生具有与日后职业生涯所必需的英语交际能力这一中心来进行，其中"实用英语"教学项目的安排与选材便是一大亮点，其主要内容均是极具实用性的应用文，如各种事务信函、广告、卡片、条据、产品介绍、求职简历等。
　　3. 加强"双基"教学，突出语言实践。坚持"应用为主、够用为度、学以致用、触类旁通"的方针，以实践为主线，理论知识点到为止。在精读课文、阅读材料、语法项目、实用英语等的教学安排上均结合学生实际，在加强学生基础知识训练的同时十分注重学生读、写、译等基础技能的训练。
　　4. 注重学生自我发展能力的培养。为此，本教程分别在精读课文和阅读材料前安排了"导学"和"导读"。这样做既方便学生课前学习，又有助于他们逐渐养成自学的习惯，从而不断增强他们这方面的能力。
　　5. 强调寓教于乐和学生文化素养的提高。"英语沙龙"便是特意为此而设立，主要内容有名人名言、谚语、短诗、幽默小品等易于上口、便于记忆而又不失风趣与教育意义的韵文。

6. 配备多媒体网络系统和电子课件。 提供图文、声音、视频等传统教程难以提供的多方位的学习资料;提供学生的个性化学习平台;提供教学内容的持续更新和动态扩展。

《新世纪应用英语教程》从教学实际出发,将传统教科书的每册10个单元改为8个单元,每个单元由五大部分组成。单元中的各组成部分不仅功能突出、特色鲜明,而且都服务于培养学生应用能力这一中心,使整个单元形成一个有机的整体,具体如下:

Part 1 课文(Text)——此为精读课文,主要为学生打好语言基础。

Part 2 语法(Grammar)——按语法项目进行较系统的专项练习,为学生语言技能的培养打基础。

Part 3 阅读(Reading)——阅读材料内容与课文(Text)的主题相关,强调知识性与趣味性。主要目的是在扩大学生词汇量的同时,开阔学生视野,加强学生阅读能力。

Part 4 实用英语(Practical English)——结合高职高专学生今后职业生涯中应用英语的实际,并根据《基本要求》中有关语言交际能力的具体要求,着重安排实用性应用文章,如信函、广告、产品介绍、个人简历等。

Part 5 英语沙龙(English Salon)——目的是寓教于乐,在提高学生文化素质的同时以潜移默化的方式加深学生对英语语言的理解。着重安排:名人名言、谚语、短诗、幽默小品文等易于上口、便于记忆,又不失幽默与教育意义的韵文。

本系列教材具有高品位和权威性,由北京大学享受两院院士级待遇的文科资深教授胡壮麟先生担任总顾问,北京大学英语系教授孙亦丽先生担任总主编,北京交通大学、重庆大学、成都大学等教学科研第一线的骨干教师参与编写工作。

本教材在编写过程中得到诸多老师和同仁的关心、指导和帮助,我们对此表示衷心感谢。除署名作者外,本书承外籍教授Paul Crutcher审阅并提出宝贵修改意见,教师黄曦、张岚和宋英等也参与了本教材的编写工作,在此一并表示感谢。但限于作者水平,加之时间紧促,如有不当之处,恳请各位读者及专家批评指正。

2005 年 10 月

目录

Unit One 1

- Part I   Text   University Life 1
- Part II   Grammar   Parts of Speech (词类) 11
- Part III   Reading Practice   College Costs in the U.S. 14
- Part IV   Practical English   Cards (卡片) I 18
- Part V   English Salon   Proverbs 20

Unit Two 21

- Part I   Text   Willis Conover and Jazz 21
- Part II   Grammar   Basic Sentence Elements
                    (基本句子成分) 30
- Part III   Reading Practice   Corning Glass Museum 32
- Part IV   Practical English   Cards (卡片) II 36
- Part V   English Salon   Tongue Twisters 39

Unit Three 40

- Part I   Text   A Sky Angel 40
- Part II   Grammar   Types of Sentences (句子类型) 51
- Part III   Reading Practice   The Stone Dog 54
- Part IV   Practical English   Notes (便条) 58
- Part V   English Salon   English Poem 62

Unit Four 63

- Part I   Text   Charles Darwin 63
- Part II   Grammar   Basic Sentence Patterns
                    (基本句型) I 74
- Part III   Reading Practice   Mark Twain 77
- Part IV   Practical English   I.O.U and Receipt
                    Forms (条据) I 81
- Part V   English Salon   Riddles 84

Unit Five ... 85

- Part I Text Home Applications of Computer Networks ... 85
- Part II Grammar Basic Sentence Patterns (基本句型) II ... 95
- Part III Reading Practice What is Cyber Love? ... 98
- Part IV Practical English Bills (单据) II ... 102
- Part V English Salon Funny Questions ... 105

Unit Six ... 106

- Part I Text Ceremonies of the Olympic Games ... 106
- Part II Grammar 基本句型转换 I Interrogative Sentences (疑问句) ... 116
- Part III Reading Practice Letter from IOC President Jacques Rogge ... 119
- Part IV Practical English Notices (通知) ... 123
- Part V English Salon English poem ... 125

Unit Seven ... 126

- Part I Text The Great Barrier Reef ... 126
- Part II Grammar 基本句型转换 II Imperative Sentences (祈使句) ... 137
- Part III Reading Practice The Great Wall ... 140
- Part IV Practical English Poster (海报) ... 144
- Part V English Salon Humorous Story ... 146

Unit Eight ... 147

- Part I Text Yellowstone National Park ... 147
- Part II Grammar 基本句型转换 III Exclamatory Sentences (感叹句) ... 157
- Part III Reading Practice Wolong Nature Reserve ... 160
- Part IV Practical English Notices (启事) ... 165
- Part V English Salon Puzzles ... 168

Vocabulary ... 169

Unit One

Part I Text

Guide to Text-Learning

1. Theme of the Text

University life is completely new to your all. What is it like? You may live on campus, manage your own time, learn in a different way and have lots of students' activities. Does it sound interesting? Read the text and see by yourself.

2. Words and Expressions Related to the Topic

schedule	进度表
lecture	演讲;讲课
deadline	最后期限
option	选修课
workload	工作量
freedom	自由
CV (curricula vitae)	(亦作:résumé)履历,简历
university life	大学生活
live on campus	住校

3. Grammatical Structures to Learn

(1) Most students **choose to live** on campus for their first year of study.
　　许多学生都宁愿在一年级时住校。

(2) **It's up to you to decide** when you'll study.
　　由你来决定什么时候要学习。

(3) You **are expected to** do a number of hours of self study.
　　你应该用很多时间来自学。

4. Grammar

Parts of Speech: Noun, Pronoun, Adjective, Adverb, Verb, Numeral, Preposition, Conjunction, Article and Interjection.

5. Practical English

Cards I: Visiting Cards/Business Cards

Warming-Up Questions:

1. What is university life like in your mind?
2. How can you be prepared for it?
3. What can you learn in the university?

University Life

1 What's university life like?

2 This is the opportunity you have been waiting for—a chance to spread your wings and enjoy new experiences. One of the best parts of university life is living away from home. You get freedom and the chance to meet new people.

3 Most students choose to live on campus for their first year of study—this usually works out cheaper than finding a flat or house and means there will definitely be loads of people in the same boat as you, so you won't feel lonely.

4 An important aspect of being at university is managing your own time. It's up to you to decide when you'll study, when you'll go shopping and when you'll

have a night out. It sounds **fantastic**, doesn't it? Of course, it's a good idea to organize your time with a weekly or monthly schedule.

5   Remember, you can be as **flexible** with your time as you like but you'll always need to make sure that you get out of bed for lectures, meet essay and project deadlines, and schedule in plenty of **review** days before exams. That's what you're here for, after all.

6   University life is about learning. You'll have anything from one to five hours of lectures, etc, in a day. But on top of that, you are expected to do a number of hours of self study.

7   At university, the way you learn may be different from at school. A stronger emphasis is placed on teaching you to **apply** information. This means, for example, being asked to answer questions where there's no right or wrong answer, but a **scope for** opinion and **debate**. You will be encouraged to read widely, to question and **analyze** what you have read, and to discuss openly your own ideas in group discussions.

8   Lectures can be given to quite large audiences, especially during the first year, or to quite small groups as in the case of students who attend **specialized** options in their final year. You are not expected to ask questions in the middle of a lecture, especially if large numbers of students are **involved**, but many lecturers will invite questions at the end.

9   If you have any problems you can speak to your lecturers and other tutors. If you plan your time and your workload, you'll have plenty of free time to enjoy student life.

10   After a hard day's study, going out and having fun is what student life is all about. A university is usually a lively city filled with events, cinemas, clubs and bars (often with great student **discounts** and special offers), so you'll never be

---

fantastic /fæn'tæstik/ *adj.*
wonderful or superb; remarkable
美好的，极妙的

flexible /'fleksəbl/ *adj.*
adaptable
可变通的；易适应的

apply /ə'plai/ *v.*
put to or adapt for a special use
应用；把……应用于

scope /skəup/ (for) *n.*
space or chance for action or thought
余地；机会

debate /di'beit/ *n.*
a discussion involving opposing points; an argument
辩论，争辩

analyze /'ænəlaiz/ *v.*
look into something deeply and thoroughly
分析

specialize /'speʃəlaiz/ *v.*
make specific mention of; particularize
特指……；限定

involve /in'vɔlv/ *v.*
engage as a participant
卷入；使参与

discount /'diskaunt/ *n.*
a reduction from the full amount of a price
折扣

short of things to do, On top of those things, there are lots of student activities to get involved in. It's the perfect way to make friends and add a bit of **sparkle** to your CV.

sparkle /'spɑːkl/ *n.*
a glittering quality
闪亮；闪光的性质

11 Students at the university are different one from another and most likely friendly, so you will feel welcome at any activity. Getting involved in a university related activity is a great way to make new friends as well.

(507 words)

Useful Phrases

choose to do sth	determine or decide to do sth	情愿；决定；认为……妥当
loads of	(informal) a lot of	大量，许多
be up to sb to do sth	to be one's responsibility to do sth	应由某人做某事
make sure that	arrange so that	确定
after all	nevertheless	毕竟；仍然
on top of	in addition to	此外
in the case of	if sth happens	在……的情况下
in the middle of	in the course of; during	在……期间
have fun	enjoy yourself	玩得开心
special offer	a low price that a store offers	特价，特价优待
be short of	have an inadequate supply of	缺乏
as well	in addition; also	另外；也

Notes

1. This is the opportunity you have been waiting for—a chance to spread your wings and enjoy new experiences. 这是一个你们梦寐以求的机会——一个可以自由自在体验新生活的机会。

you have been waiting for 定语从句修饰 opportunity,关系代词 that 省略了。

2. An important aspect of being at university is managing your own time. 上大学的一大特点就是可以自主安排时间。

being at university 为动名词短语作介词宾语;managing your own time 为动名词短语作主语补足语(即传统语法中的表语)。

3. A university is usually a lively city filled with events, cinemas, clubs and bars (often with great student discounts and special offers), so you'll never be short of things to do, on top of which, there are lots of student activities to get involved in. 大学校园就是一座生机勃勃的城市,其中有各种各样的社交活动,有电影院、俱乐部,还有酒吧(学生们常常还可以享受折扣和优惠),因此学生们不会无所事事,此外还有很多学生活动可供参加。

on top of which 引导一个非限制性定语从句。

Reading Aloud and Memorizing the Following

I. Read the following paragraph taken from the text until you learn it by heart.

At university, the way you learn may be different from at school. A stronger emphasis is placed on teaching you to apply information. This means, for example, being asked to answer questions where there's no right or wrong answer, but scope for opinion and debate. You will be encouraged to read widely, to question and analyze what you have read, and to discuss openly your own ideas in group discussions.

Comprehension of the Text

II. Choose the best answer to each of the following questions according to the passage.

1. According to the passage, most university students would like to live on campus because _____.
   A. it will cost less money
   B. they can live alone
   C. they can do a lot of self study
   D. they can spread their wings and enjoy their new experiences

2. The difference between a university and a school lies in that _____.
   A. you can't ask questions during a lecture
   B. you have to get out of bed for lectures
   C. you will be given more room for discussion and debate
   D. you will have a lot of homework

3. The writer of the passage intends to give some advice to _____.
   A. freshmen   B. sophomores   C. juniors   D. seniors

4. The more activities you have taken part in during your university time, the more you can add to your _____.
   A. report   B. study   C. essay   D. resume

5. The most important part of university life is _____.
   A. organizing your time
   B. learning
   C. applying information
   D. being asked to answer questions

III. Answer the following questions with the information you've got from the text.

1. What kind of chance have you been waiting for?   (Para. 2)
2. How can you organize your time?   (Para. 4)
3. Why should you make sure to get out of bed for lectures?   (Para. 5)
4. What will you be encouraged to do at university?   (Para. 7)
5. If you plan your time well, you will have plenty of free time, won't you?

Vocabulary

IV. Find the definition in column B which matches the words or expressions in column A.

A	B
1. schedule	( ) a. a lot of
2. scope	( ) b. of or relating to a week
3. opportunity	( ) c. lack
4. have fun	( ) d. teacher
5. be short of	( ) e. wonderful
6. lecturer	( ) f. plan
7. weekly	( ) g. chance
8. fantastic	( ) h. should
9. be expected to	( ) i. room
10. plenty of	( ) j. have a good time

V. Fill in the blanks with the words given in the brackets. Change the form where necessary.

1. We have the _____ to do as we please all afternoon. (free)
2. The first message is _____ to arrive at 7 o'clock this evening. (expect)
3. A _____ paper is printed every month. (month)
4. The shop _____ in mountain-climbing equipment. (special)
5. He has just been back from a _____ trip to Europe. (fantastic)
6. The teacher _____ the student to enter the competition. (courage)
7. They interviewed _____ members of the community. (difference)
8. A _____ person is full of life and is always doing things. (life)
9. Too many extracurricular _____ take up too much of our precious time for study. (active)
10. They give 10% _____ for cash payment. (count)

VI. Complete each of the following sentences with the most appropriate word or words from the four choices marked A, B, C and D.

1. Several students are _____ from school because of illness.
   A. way   B. late   C. away   D. down
2. There's plenty of scope _____ improvement in his work.
   A. to   B. for   C. on   D. of
3. His father placed great hopes _____ him.
   A. on   B. to   C. for   D. of
4. He chooses _____ into the matter till the truth is out.
   A. looking   B. looked   C. looks   D. to look
5. I'm short _____ money this week. Can you lend me some?
   A. for   B. up   C. of   D. from
6. Please add a few more names of students _____ the list.
   A. to   B. into   C. up   D. for
7. It is _____ you to decide whether to go or not.
   A. away from   B. up to   C. in front of   D. into
8. I believe that you can work _____ this problem by yourself.
   A. in   B. up   C. on   D. out
9. The next thing on our _____ is to telephone our friends.
   A. schedule   B. scheme   C. school   D. scholar
10. I hope we can finish the project before the _____.
   A. date   B. time   C. deadline   D. plan

Structure

VII. Rewrite the following sentences after the models.

Model 1   He'd like to go to work by bike.

 go to work by bike.

1. She did not want to accept my present.
2. I would like to say nothing.
3. He didn't want to help me.
4. How she would like to live is none of my business.

5. I preferred to remain an onlooker during their quarrel.

Model 2   You should get the work done.
          It's up to you to get the work done.

1. We should give them all the help we can.
2. Parents should teach their children manners.
3. You should break the news to him.
4. You had to tell her about her failure in the exam.
5. You should make the change.

VIII. Study the model and translate the following sentences into English.

Model   You are expected to work late if you are needed to.

1. 你应该在此多呆一些时候。
2. 海伦应该尽快回来。
3. 你不应该这样说。
4. 他不应该这么快就做出决定。
5. 要想提高阅读水平,你应该多读一些书。

Translation

IX. Translate the following sentences into Chinese.

1. This usually works out cheaper than finding a flat or house and means there will definitely be loads of people in the same boat as you, so you won't feel lonely.

2. An important aspect of being at university is managing your own time.

3. It's a good idea to organize your time with a weekly or monthly schedule.

4. You can be as flexible with your time as you like.

5. This means, for example, being asked to answer questions where there's no right or wrong answer, but scope for opinion and debate.

X. Translate the following sentences into English using the words or phrases in the brackets.

1. 所有的孩子都参加了学校排练的话剧。(involve)

2. 他们在假期里举办了大量聚会。(loads of)

3. 一定让他记下来。(make sure)

4. 除此以外,还有其他几项好处。(on top of)

5. 我知道他未完成这项工作,不过,他已经尽力了。(after all)

Part II Grammar

Parts of Speech（词类）

根据词的意义及其在句中的功能将词分为若干类,叫做词类。英语的词通常分为十大类:

英语名称	汉译	作 用	例 词
Noun (*n.*)	名 词	表示人、事物、地点或抽象概念的名称	pen, Beijing
Pronoun (*pron.*)	代 词	代替名词或名词短语	we, each
Adjective (*adj.*)	形容词	说明人或事物的性质或特征	great, black
Adverb (*adv.*)	副 词	表示动作或状态的特征或程度	quickly, often
Verb (*v.*)	动 词	表示动作或状态	go, contain
Numeral (*num.*)	数 词	表示数目或顺序	five, eighth
Preposition (*prep.*)	介 词	用于名词或代词前,说明它与其他句子成分之间的关系	in, with
Conjunction (*conj.*)	连 词	连接词、短语、从句或句子	but, whether
Article (*art.*)	冠 词	位于名词前,用来说明名词所指的人或事物	a(n), the
Interjection (*int.*)	感叹词	表示喜怒哀乐等感情	oh, ah

属于前六类的词(名、代、形、副、动、数)都有实义,叫做实词(Notional Word),它们在句中可单独充当句子成分,在句中一般要重读(代词除外)。

后四类词(介、连、冠、感叹)没有实义,叫做虚词(Form Word)。介词、连词和冠词在句中不能独立充当句子成分,在句中一般不重读。感叹词在结构上常被看成独立成分,在句中通常重读。

I. Complete each of the following sentences with the most appropriate word or words from the four choices marked A, B, C and D.

1. I'm old enough to wash _____ clothes by myself. You can just wash _____.
   A. my, your   B. mine, yours   C. my, yours   D. your, my

2. The father wished the twins to be doctors, but _____ of them liked to study medicine.
   A. both   B. neither   C. either   D. none

3. We are doing much better _____ English _____ our teachers' help.
   A. in, at   B. at, in   C. in, with   D. with, with

4. —Dad, when will you be free? You agreed to go to the seaside with me four days ago.
   —I am sorry, Jean. But I think I will have a _____ holiday soon.
   A. four-days   B. four-day   C. four days   D. four day

5. A _____ argument on any dispute is beneficial to the further understanding of the mutual views.
   A. friend   B. friended   C. friendly   D. friendless

6. It was too hard for me to figure out _____ he meant.
   A. what   B. that   C. when   D. why

7. Cars and buses _____ stop when the traffic lights turn red.
   A. can   B. need   C. may   D. must

8. John fell asleep _____ he was listening to the music.
   A. after   B. before   C. while   D. as soon as

9. We should _____ a theory to practice.
   A. supply   B. apply   C. use   D. request

10. _____ hard-working a student he is!
    A. What   B. How   C. That   D. Very

II. Tell what part of speech the italicized word in each sentence is.

1. What's university life *like*?
2. One of the best parts of university life is living *away* from home.
3. It's up *to* you to decide when you'll study, when you'll go shopping and when you'll have a night out.
4. That's *what* you're here for.
5. A university is usually a *lively* city filled with events, cinemas, clubs and bars.
6. A stronger *emphasis* is placed on teaching you to apply information.
7. —Do you know anything about the Great Wall?
   —*Why*, of course.
8. It *sounds* fantastic, doesn't it?

III. Fill in the blanks with the words given in the box in their proper forms.

| break | far | old | interest | apply |
| thank | fool | ever | German | either |

1. So far, no man has travelled _____ than the moon.
2. How _____ the film is!
3. He is _____ enough to believe that man.
4. The old man was very _____.
5. You have _____ lost a book before, have you?
6. Mary is the _____ of the three girls in the family.
7. Could you lend me your ruler? Mine is _____.
8. The girl was not born in _____.

Part III Reading Practice

Guide to Reading

1. Words and Expressions to Learn

cost	n.	成本;价钱;代价
average	adj.	一般的;通常的;平均的
differ	v.	不一致,不同
rate	n.	比率;速度;等级;价格,费用
increase	v. & n.	增加,加大
point out		指出
public college		公立学院
financial aid		财政援助
in the form of		以……的形式
College Board		学院董事会
private college		[美]私立学院
the American Council on Education		美国教育委员会

2. Pre-Reading Questions

(1) Is there any grant system in China?

(2) How much do you pay for tuition each year?

College Costs in the U. S.

1   A new report said the cost of studies at public colleges in the United States increased fourteen percent this year. This is the biggest increase in **tuition** (*n.* 学费) in thirty years. But the study also found that the average student paid a lot less than the published costs of a college education, because of **grants** (*n.* 助学金). And it pointed out that American students received a record amount of financial aid last year.

2   Students do not have to repay grants, unlike financial aid in the form of **loans** (*n.* 贷款). About half of American college students receive grants. This means that education costs differ from student to student.

3   The report is from the College Board. This is a non-profit membership group of schools and other educational organizations. One of its best-known jobs is to administer college entrance tests. The College Board said tuition at two-year public colleges rose at the same rate as four-year schools.

4   The College Board said the increases were mainly caused by **cuts** (*n.* 削减) in state spending on education. But a **congressman** (*n.* 国会议员) says colleges have increased their prices in both good and bad economic times. John Boehner of Ohio is chairman of the House Committee on Education and the Work Force. He says colleges do not want to talk about their decisions to spend money to build things like **rock-climbing** (*n.* 攀岩) walls.

5   The College Board collected information from four-thousand colleges and universities. It says the average total charge for students who live at a public college in their state is ten-thousand-six-hundred dollars. While tuition rose fourteen percent this year, housing and other costs increased at a lower rate.

6   At a private college, total charges are almost twenty-seven-thousand dollars.

That is an increase of about six percent over last year.

7   David Ward is president of the American Council on Education. His group represents colleges and universities. Mr. Ward called the College Board findings bad news. But he says percentage increases in tuition do not tell the whole story. He says there is good news about grants and other student aid.

8   The College Board said financial aid for the last school year reached 105,000 million dollars. That amount was up **sharply** (*ad.* 急剧地) from the year before.

Reading Comprehension

I. Answer the following questions according to the passage.

1. How much did the cost of studies at public colleges in the United States increase this year according to the report?
2. The students do not have to pay the financial aid in the form of loans, do they?
3. What is one of the best jobs of the College Board?
4. How much are the total charges for a student at a private college?
5. Why does Mr. Ward say percentage increases in tuition do not tell the whole story?

II. Translate into Chinese the following sentences taken from the passage.

1. A new report said the cost of studies at public colleges in the United States increased fourteen percent this year.
2. And it pointed out that American students received a record amount of financial aid last year.
3. The College Board said tuition at two-year public colleges rose at the same rate as four-year schools.
4. It says the average total charge for students who live at a public college in their state is ten-thousand-six-hundred dollars.

5. But he says percentage increases in tuition do not tell the whole story.

III. **Fill in the blanks with the words or phrases listed in Words and Expressions to Learn. Change the form where necessary.**

1. The birth _____ decreased by 0.03% last year.
2. The campus is _____ from what it was 20 years ago.
3. He did not put it in the _____ of a question.
4. He _____ out that the road was not safe in winter.
5. He saved his daughter at the _____ of his life.
6. What is the _____ rainfall for August in your country?
7. His employer has _____ his wages.
8. An English-Chinese Dictionary is an important _____ for learning English.

IV. **Complete the following sentences.**

1. Giving advice at the right time has to _____ (需要人的睿智).
2. We give _____ (九折优惠) for cash.
3. He _____ (专门研究) oriental history.
4. The manager received twenty _____ (求职申请书).
5. _____ (不仅借了我 50 英镑), he asked me to lend him my car.
6. _____ (一笔贷款) would help me out of my predicament.
7. There was _____ (不断增长) in population.
8. Mary has derived a lot of benefit _____ (从她的教学中).

Part IV Practical English

Cards（卡片）I

Visiting Cards / Business Cards（名片）

在社交活动中，交换名片是一项很流行、也很重要的活动。名片的书写要规范，符合语言表达规则。名片通常包括八个部分：

1. 公司名称 (name of the company)
2. 本人姓名 (person's name)
3. 职位、职称、头衔 (position or title)
4. 公司地址 (address of the company)
5. 邮政编码 (post code)
6. 电话号码 (telephone number)
7. 传真号码 (fax number)
8. 电子邮箱 (E-mail address)

如：

MING YING ELECTRONIC EQUIPMENT COMPANY

Chen Mingyue

Sales Assistant

No. 26, Daxi Road, Haidian District   Fax: 010-86081514
Beijing 100510, P.R.China   Tel: 010-86081515
E-mail: chmy@sohu.com

明瑛电子设备公司

陈 明 岳

销售助理

地址：中国北京市海淀区大西路 26 号　　传真：010-86081514

邮编：100510　　　　　　　　　　　　　电话：010-86081515

电子邮件：chmy@sohu.com

Useful Expressions

General Manager	总经理
Business Manager	业务经理
Vice Manager	副经理
Secretary to the Manager	经理秘书
Computer Engineer	电脑工程师
Chief Adviser	首席顾问
Purchasing Manager	采购经理
Quality-Control Engineer	质检工程师
Manager of Export Section	出口部经理

Exercises

按照英语名片格式给成都星海集团（Chengdu Xinghai Groups）出口部经理张洪海设计一张名片。

地址：四川省成都市人民路 168 号　　传真：028-4567886

邮编：610015　　　　　　　　　　　　电话：028-4567888

电子邮件：zhh@163.com

Part V English Salon

Proverbs

A good beginning is half done.
良好的开端是成功的一半。
A good book is a good friend.
好书如挚友。
A good book is the best of friends, the same today and forever.
一本好书,相伴一生。
All things are difficult before they are easy.
万事开头难。
Constant dripping wears away the stone.
锲而不舍,金石可镂。

Requirement

Try to collect more English proverbs and communicate with your partner.

Unit Two

Part I Text

Guide to Text-Learning

1. Theme of the Text

   Perhaps you like jazz music very much, but how much do you know about jazz music? Who helps make jazz music an international language?

2. Words and Expressions Related to the Topic

guitarist	吉他弹奏者
broadcast	广播，播音
announcer	播音员
jazz musician	爵士乐音乐家
racial separation	种族隔离
Washington, D.C.	(美国首都)哥伦比亚特区华盛顿

3. Grammatical Structures to Learn

(1) Willis **had an interview with** the great Duke Ellington.

   威利斯会见了赫赫有名的埃林顿公爵。

(2) Though his programs are **no longer** broadcast, his influence is very much alive.

   虽然他的节目不再播放了，但他的影响却长存于世。

(3) Jazz music **owes a great deal to** this special man.

   爵士乐归功于这个不同寻常的人。

4. Grammar

Basic Sentence Elements: Subject, Predict, Predictive, Object, Adverbial and Attribute.

21

5. Practical English

Cards II: Cards of Greetings and Congratulations; Cards of Sending Gifts

Warming-Up Questions:

1. What music do you like best?
2. How much do you know about jazz music?
3. In which country is jazz music famous?

Willis Conover and Jazz

1   Willis Conover was not a jazz musician. However, many people believed that he did more to spread the sound of jazz than any other person in music history. For more than forty years Willis brought jazz to people around the world on his VOA music programs, helping make jazz music an **international** language.

2   When Willis was in high school, he played the part of a radio announcer in a school play. Later, he took part in a spelling **competition** that was broadcast on radio. The radio announcer told Willis that he should work in radio because of his deep and rich voice that was **perfect** for broadcasting. Later, Willis became a real radio announcer and worked for several radio stations.

3   Willis heard a lot of jazz music during the 1940s in Washington, D.C. which was the center of a very important jazz movement. Willis knew many of the jazz musicians in both Washington

---

international /ˌɪntə(ː)ˈnæʃənəl/ *adj.*
global
国际的,世界的

competition /ˌkɒmpɪˈtɪʃən/ *n.*
contest
竞赛

perfect /ˈpɜːfɪkt/ *adj.*
excellent
完美的,理想的

and New York City. He helped organize many concerts and stop racial separation. Willis **created** musical events where people of all races were welcome. Willis once said that jazz was the music of freedom and that with jazz people could express their lives through music which helped them to stand up a little straighter.

4   During years of his program, Willis **presented** his expert knowledge about jazz. He interviewed great jazz musicians such as Duke Ellington and Louis Armstrong and played the best music from the most **current** musicians. Willis not only talked about jazz music on his program, but wrote the music and the words to jazz songs, especially sad love songs.

5   Audiences loved his program. When he traveled to Poland in 1959, he saw hundreds of people gathered near his plane. With cameras and flowers, they were cheering and smiling. Willis thought that they were waiting for somebody to arrive. Then, he saw a large **sign** that read, "Welcome to Poland, Mister Conover."—the crowds were there to see him. Willis also worked to spread jazz in the United States. He was the announcer for many famous jazz festivals and concerts in America. He presented more than thirty concerts at the John F. Kennedy Center for the Performing Arts in Washington, D. C. He even produced the White House concert in celebration of jazz musician Duke Ellington's seventieth birthday in 1969.

6   Willis once said that Louis Armstrong was the heart of jazz, Duke Ellington was the soul and Count Basie was its happy dancing feet. In 1973, Willis had an **interview** with the great Duke Ellington. This was one of the last times Conover talked to him. In this interview, these great men expressed their thanks to one another.

7   Willis died in 1996 after a long struggle with cancer. Though his programs are no longer broadcast, his influence is very much alive. Jazz music owes a great deal to this special man.

(479 words)

---

create /kri'eit/ v.
cause to exist; bring into being
创造,创作
present /pri'zent/ v.
show or display
介绍;给;上演;呈现
current /'kʌrənt/ adj.
belonging to the present time
当前的,现在的,最近的
sign /sain/ n.
mark, symbol, etc. used to represent sth
标记,符号;征兆,迹象;标牌,招牌
interview /'intəvju:/ n.
a formal meeting in person
接见,会见

Useful Phrases

the center of	the core of	……的中心
such as	for example	例如
have an interview with	meet with	会见……
no longer	not any more	不再
owe...to	feel grateful to	感谢,归功于

Notes

1. jazz(爵士乐),源于20世纪初期美国新奥尔良一带,是民间音乐、流行音乐、古典音乐的融合。它至少是由两股潮流演变发展而来,一是美国黑人在音乐上的创造性的贡献——Ragtime 和 Blues;其二是一些已有的音乐形式(当时的流行音乐、进行曲、四对舞曲等等)。
2. Duke Ellington (1899–1974): American popular jazz musician
3. Louis Armstrong(1901–1971): American popular jazz musician
4. stand up a little straighter: 挺直腰

Exercises

Reading Aloud and Memorizing the Following

1. Read the following paragraph taken from the text until you learn it by heart.

Willis Conover was not a jazz musician. However, many people believed that he did more to spread the sound of jazz than any other person in music history. For more than forty years Willis brought jazz to people around world on his music programs, helping make jazz music an international language.

Comprehension of the Text

II. Choose the best answer to each of the following questions according to the passage.

1. According to the passage, Willis Conover helped make jazz music an international language because _____.
   A. he made jazz music an international language
   B. he broadcast jazz around the world
   C. he helped organize many concerts
   D. people can express their lives with jazz

2. Willis Conover obtained his knowledge of jazz _____.
   A. in high school   B. from Washington, D.C.
   C. from New York City   D. from radio stations

3. The writer of the passage intends to tell us Willis Conover was a great _____.
   A. jazz musician   B. guitarist
   C. musician   D. announcer

4. Willis Conover's great wish was _____.
   A. to see the world in peace   B. to spread jazz in America
   C. to be remembered and respected   D. to make jazz popular around the world

5. Though his programs are no longer broadcast, his influence is _____.
   A. full of life   B. successful   C. great   D. deep

III. Answer the following questions with the information you've got from the text.

1. Why did Willis choose to work in radio stations?   (Para. 2)
2. Do you agree to Willis' saying that jazz is the music of freedom?   (Para. 3)
3. How did people react when they heard of Willis' arrival?   (Para. 5)
4. How did Willis comment on Louis Armstrong?   (Para. 6)
5. Name some of his contributions to Jazz music.

Vocabulary

IV. Find the definition in column B which matches the words or expressions in column A.

A	B
1. influence	( ) a. show
2. voice	( ) b. happening now
3. spread	( ) c. contest
4. present	( ) d. be known by many people
5. competition	( ) e. affect
6. current	( ) f. assemble
7. announcer	( ) g. flawless
8. perfect	( ) h. speak out
9. take part in	( ) i. broadcaster
10. gather	( ) j. participate in

V. Fill in the blanks with the words given in the brackets. Change the form where necessary.

1. Graduates have to fight for jobs in a highly _____ market. (compete)
2. Some people argue that the present evaluation and grading system at college is set up against the growth of students' _____. (create)
3. The document was signed in the _____ of two witnesses. (present)
4. She was forced to _____ on the check. (sign)
5. They have pledged to end _____ discrimination in such areas as employment. (race)
6. The tournament is _____ to players under the age of 20. (restriction)
7. The new management techniques aim to improve _____. (perform)
8. My time spent in the library was very _____. (produce)
9. The qualification has gained _____ all over the world. (current)
10. Their music has become very _____ in recent years. (commercial)

VI. Complete each of the following sentences with the most appropriate word or words from the four choices marked A, B, C and D.

1. To _____ the freedom of press is not advisable.
   A. limit   B. confine   C. restrict   D. restriction

2. The students took up the study of medicine under the _____ of a high-school biology teacher.
   A. effect   B. influence   C. affect   D. affection

3. We can't compete _____ them _____ price.
   A. with, on   B. with, for   C. against, for   D. against, in

4. His argument simply doesn't _____ close examination.
   A. stand up   B. stand up for   C. stand up to   D. stand out

5. Dumplins are _____ Chinese.
   A. popular with   B. welcome by
   C. popular for   D. welcomed with

6. He was _____ pleased to know that his application for the position was accepted.
   A. not more than   B. more than
   C. no more than   D. less than

7. Now I've realized that my _____ of her character was one-sided.
   A. estimate   B. evaluation   C. value   D. appraisement

8. The local residents launched a campaign to _____ funds for the homeless.
   A. raise   B. gather   C. organize   D. collect

9. In this city, many rules and regulations have racial meanings: they are _____ the colored.
   A. set up   B. set out for   C. set up against   D. set off

10. It was a _____ broadcast, not a recording.
    A. alive   B. lively   C. liven   D. live

Structure

VII. Rewrite the following sentences after the models.

Model 1   He said his success was due to hard work and good luck.

He owed his success to hard work and good luck.

1. She can speak fluent English with regular practice.
2. She is in good health because she has been going on a diet and having exercises.
3. They had a good harvest. They said it was because of fine weather.
4. Thanks to advanced technology, we can communicate with people all over the world conveniently now.
5. Without government's support, their experiment wouldn't have been so successful.

Model 2   I don't want to wait in vain any longer.

I no longer want to wait in vain.

1. You've grown up, so stop behaving like a child.
2. She didn't insist on his wearing a suit any longer.
3. The child had outgrown the skirt.
4. We disbelieve his words from now on.
5. He has given up smoking.

VIII. Study the model and translate the following sentences into English.

Model   He had an interview with a career adviser.

1. 导演会见了那位电影明星。
2. 他会见了一位著名的心理学家。
3. 部长就环境问题接见了记者。
4. 新首相接见了内阁(cabinet)成员。
5. 当地政府官员接见了来访的学者们。

Translation

IX. Translate the following sentences into Chinese.

1. Willis once said that jazz was the music of freedom and that with jazz people could express their lives through music which helped them to stand up a little straighter.

2. However, many people believed that he did more to spread the sound of jazz than any other person in music history.

3. The radio announcer told Willis that he should work in radio because of his deep and rich voice that was perfect for broadcasting.

4. Willis created musical events where people of all races were welcome.

5. Willis Conover once said that Louis Armstrong was the heart of jazz, Duke Ellington was the soul and Count Basie was its happy dancing feet.

X. Translate the following sentences into English using the words or phrases in the brackets.

1. 老师在教学中应鼓励学生充分发表自己的见解,在考试中充分发挥想象。(voice)

2. 很难估计有多少人在山洪中遇难。(estimate)

3. 小孩通常都会在母亲面前争宠。(compete)

4. 关于他辞职的谣言迅速传播开来。(spread)

5. 父母对孩子们沉溺于电脑游戏的现象表示担忧。(express)

Part II Grammar

Basic Sentence Elements（基本句子成分）

成分	概念	举例
主语	一句的主体，全句述说的对象，常用名词或相当于名词的短语或从句担任，一般位于句首。	1. **I** work for that factory. 2. **He** was proud of his son.
谓语	说明主语的动作或状态，常用动词担任，一般位于主语之后。	1. He **lacks** patience. 2. We **put** the book on the table.
表语	在系动词后所必须添加的词、短语或从句。这种添加部分不是该动词的动作承受者，而只是对其表意的一种必不可少的补充，是对主语的一种说明或描述。	1. She is **beautiful**. 2. He looks **miserable**.
宾语	表示及物动词的动作对象和介词所联系的对象，常由名词或相当于名词的词、短语或从句担任，一般置于及物动词或介词之后。	1. They are singing **a song**. 2. I love **my country**.
状语	是修饰动词、形容词、副词以及全句的，常由副词或相当于副词的短语或从句担任。修饰动词时，可置于动词之前或之后；修饰形容词或副词时，常置于它们之前。	1. **Suddenly**, he said something unexpected. 2. He got up **late**.
定语	是限定或修饰名词或相当于名词的词，常由形容词或相当于形容词的短语或从句担任。形容词常置于名词之前，相当于形容词的短语或从句常置于名词之后。	1. She has a **lovely** son. 2. It's a **beautiful** garden.

 **Exercises**

I. Tell the sentence elements of the following sentences.

1. For more than forty years, Willis brought jazz to people around the world on his VOA music programs.
2. People told him that he sounded like a real radio announcer.
3. He had full freedom to play all kinds of jazz music on his show which began in 1955.
4. Willis thought that they were waiting for somebody to arrive.
5. He was the announcer for many famous jazz festivals and concerts in America.

II. Underline the sentence elements according to the requirements.

1. Later, he took part in a spelling competition that was broadcast on radio.(主语、宾语、状语)
2. Willis knew that he had found a perfect job.(谓语、宾语、定语)
3. He was the announcer for many famous jazz festivals and concerts in America. (表语、定语)
4. Willis once said that Louis Armstrong was the heart of jazz.(状语、宾语、表语)
5. In the entrance to the museum there is a sculpture by a famous American glass artist named Dale Chihuly.(主语、定语、状语)

III. Fill in the blanks with the words given in the box in their proper forms.

| know | whether | fix | though | also |
| that | necessity | ever | where | from |

1. It is very _____ that we should develop education in the countryside.
2. _____ he is coming or not doesn't matter too much.
3. Who did the work is _____.
4. My idea is _____ we should help her do housework every Sunday.
5. It is not yet _____ when the parent-teacher meeting will be held.
6. Everyone wants to visit the place _____ Premier Zhou once worked.
7. Please tell me _____ whom you borrowed the English novel.
8. The cadre often goes in among the masses, _____ he is very old.

Part III Reading Practice

Guide to Reading

1. Words and Expressions to Learn

substance	n.	物质
artwork	n.	艺术品,美术品
exhibit	v.	展出,陈列
resist	v.	抵抗,反抗;忍得住
container	n.	容器(箱、盆、罐、壶、桶、坛子);集装箱
manufacture	v.	制造,加工
	n.	制造,制造业;产品
chemical	adj.	化学的
	n.	化学制品,化学药品
crystal	adj.	结晶状的
	n.	水晶,水晶饰品;结晶,晶体
demonstration	n.	示范,实证
device	n.	装置,设备;设计;图案;策略;发明物
Internet	n.	因特网,国际互联网络,网际网

2. Pre-Reading Questions

(1) Can you imagine what our life would be like without glass?
(2) How much do you know about glass?

Corning Glass Museum

1   Do you know that glass is both a liquid and a solid? Or that glass is one of the oldest **substances** (*n.* 物质) made by humans? These are some of the many interesting facts that visitors can learn at the Corning Museum of Glass in Corning, New York.

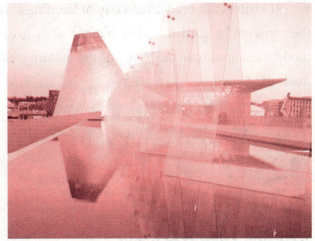

2   The Corning Museum of Glass has one of the largest and most important glass collections in the world. Visitors can see many beautiful objects. These include three-thousand-year-old glass animals from **Egypt** (*n.* 埃及), finely made European drinking glasses, and works by modern glass artists from all over the world.

3   In the entrance to the museum there is a **sculpture** (*n.* 雕塑) by a famous American glass artist named Dale Chihuly. This artwork is more than three meters tall and made of five hundred pieces of wildly-shaped green glass. The sculpture looks more like a living sea creature than a glass object!

4   However, the Corning Museum of Glass is not just for pieces of art, there are also many exhibits that explain the science of glass. For example, you can learn about an important glass discovery that was made more than ninety years ago. In 1913, a scientist discovered that putting the chemical **boric oxide** (硼氧化物) into glass made it able to resist high temperatures. With the help of his wife, this scientist invented **Pyrex** (*n.* 耐热玻璃), special glass containers made for cooking. In fact, Pyrex used to be manufactured in the Corning factory near the current Museum of Glass.

5   The technology of glass is very important in other ways that you might not think about. For example, glass is necessary to make **fiber optic cables** (光纤电缆), devices that make the Internet connections possible. Glass is even used to make

LCDs, or liquid crystal displays. These technologies are used for manufacturing television and computer screens.

6   Visitors to the museum can also take part in glass activities. Every few hours an expert gives a glass-blowing demonstration. Using a steel pole, the expert forms hot liquid glass into a cup or **vase** (*n.* 花瓶). There is even a special area where visitors can make their own glass objects.

7   If visitors are tired after a day of learning about glass, they can enjoy a meal in the museum's garden. This outside area gives people a chance to enjoy the modern **architecture** (*n.* 建筑) of the building. Can you guess what the building is made of? Glass!

Reading Comprehension

I. Answer the following questions according to the passage.

1. Why is the Corning Museum of Glass so famous?
2. What kind of glass did people discover about 100 years ago?
3. What role does glass play in modern technology?
4. What activities can visitors take part in?
5. Where can you enjoy your meal when you feel tired?

II. Translate into Chinese the following sentences taken from the passage.

1. The sculpture looks more like a living sea creature than a glass object!
2. In fact, Pyrex used to be manufactured in the Corning factory near the current Museum of Glass.
3. The technology of glass is very important in other ways that you might not think about.
4. However, the Corning Museum of Glass is not just for pieces of art, there are also many exhibits that explain the science of glass.

5. Can you guess what the building is made of?

III. Fill in the blanks with the words or phrases listed in Words and Expressions to Learn. Change the form where necessary.

1. She couldn't _____ making jokes about his strange clothes.
2. Whisky _____ a large percentage of alcohol.
3. How would you _____ that men evolves from apes?
4. New models of mobile phones are _____ at the annual Guangzhou Trade Fair.
5. Water, ice and snow are the same _____ in different forms.
6. He invented a new _____ for catching mice.
7. He majors in _____ because he dreams of becoming a _____ when he grows up.
8. The numbers on the products indicate the _____ of the goods.

IV. Complete the following sentences.

1. They _____ (建了一座新城市) where there was only desert before.
2. We _____ (把一切成就归功于) the wise leadership of our Party.
3. The chairman _____ (会见了) the reporter.
4. He has the power _____ (抵抗疾病).
5. _____ (在老师的帮助下), I passed the final examination.
6. We _____ (过去常常参加劳动) in that commune.
7. Janet _____ (收集了许多很好的) foreign stamps.
8. It _____ (好像) they will win the election.

Part IV   Practical English

Cards（卡片）II

1. Cards of Greetings and Congratulations（贺卡）

贺卡的种类很多，有生日卡、圣诞卡、新年卡、结婚纪念卡等等。通常，贺卡抬头写被祝贺人的姓名（姓名前可加"to"，亦可不加），结尾签祝贺人的姓名（姓名前可加"from"，亦可不加），贺卡的信封可封也可不封，寄卡人不需写出自己的地址。

如：

>
> **To Mr. and Mrs. W. Dean**
>
> With Best Wishes
>
> for
>
> A Merry Christmas
>
> and
>
> A Happy New Year
>
> *From Mr. and Mrs. Healey*

>
> 致迪恩先生及夫人
>
> 圣诞快乐
>
> 新年愉悦
>
> 并致以最衷心的祝愿
>
> 希利先生及夫人谨祝

2. Cards of Sending Gifts（赠物卡）

人们常为表达祝贺和谢意而赠送礼物，为了更好地表达情谊，可在卡片上写上赠语，附在礼物上一并送出。此谓赠物卡。赠物卡用语应简洁，真诚，需说明受礼人、送礼缘由、送礼人三方面内容。

如：

Sept. 10th, 05

Dear Frank,

    I want to send you this alarm clock because I know you need it to wake you up for your morning shift. And it will help you get up on time with no hurry in the morning.

Yours,
Henry

亲爱的弗兰克，

    我想送这个闹钟给你是因为我知道你需要它在上早班的时候叫醒你，而且它能使你早上不至于慌忙。

亨利
2005.9.10

Useful Expressions

Best wishes on this holiday season.	致以节日最诚挚的祝福。
A merry Christmas and a happy new year.	圣诞快乐，恭贺新禧。
I determine to present...	我打算送……
Congratulations on your... (graduation, achievement, promotion, new job, etc.)	祝贺你……（毕业、有成就、升职、跳槽成功等等）

Exercises

I. Fill in the blanks in the following English greeting so that it is functionally equivalent to the Chinese version.

亲爱的妈妈:

　　我刚刚邮寄了一份礼物。希望它能赶在母亲节到您手上。祝您母亲节快乐。我希望能与您一起分享。

　　　　　　　　　　　　　　　　　　　　玛丽

Dear Mum,

　　I just put a gift into the mail. I hope it _____ _____. Have a very happy Mother's Day. I wish _____ _____ with you.

　　　　　　　　　　　　　　　　　　　　Mary

II. Write a card to congratulate your uncle John and aunt Sophia for their new baby.

Part V English Salon

Tongue Twisters

She sells sea shells by the sea shore.
The shells she sells are surely sea shells.
So if she sells shells on the sea shore.
I'm sure she sells sea shore shells.

Peter Piper picked a peck of pickled peppers.
A peck of pickled peppers did Peter Piper pick.
If Peter Piper picked a peck of pickled peppers.
Where's the peck of pickled peppers Peter Piper picked?

If one doctor doctors another doctor,
Does the doctor who doctors the doctor
Doctor the doctor the way the doctor is doctoring doctors?
Or does he doctor the doctor the way the doctor who doctors the doctors?

Requirement

Work in pairs and see who can read faster and more clearly.

Unit Three

Part I Text

Guide to Text-Learning

1. Theme of the Text

   Many girls dream of becoming a flight attendant. But does it only mean a high pay and colorful life? What is the responsibility of a flight attendant? How will you respond and react properly to unexpected incidences? And how can you be called a sky angel? Read the text and see by yourself.

2. Words and Expressions Related to the Topic

adventure	冒险,奇遇
angel	天使
aircraft	飞机,飞行器
cabin	船舱,飞机舱
crew	全体乘务员
culmination	极点,顶点
diaper	一次性尿布
destination	目的地
lavatory	(有抽水马桶的)厕所
onboard	装载于……的
romance	罗曼史,浪漫
wing	(鸟的)翅膀;机翼;飞行徽章
flight attendant	空乘人员
coach cabin	教练飞行舱

3. Grammatical Structures to Learn

(1) They brought cloth towels from first class to assist in cleaning up both mom and the infant.

她们从头等舱拿来了毛巾帮着给那位妈妈和她的婴儿清洁。

(2) And each time I see them, I am reminded of that young woman.

每次我看见他们,我就想起了那位年轻的女士。

(3) With tears in my eyes I gave her a hug and told her...

我的眼泪涌了出来,拥抱着她说道……

4. Grammar

Types of Sentences: Simple sentence, Compound sentence and Complex sentence.

5. Practical English

Notes: Asking for leave; Message Left

Warming-Up Questions:

1. What's your impression of a flight attendant?
2. What do you think is the duty of a flight attendant?

A Sky Angel

1 In 1978, I became a flight attendant for a major airline. Earning my wings was the **culmination** of a childhood dream that I had set for myself after my first plane ride at the age of five. Like so many others before me, I fell in love with the romance of airplanes, adventure and helping others.

2 I have flown hundreds of flights since graduation, but one stands out among the many.

3 We were flying from Los Angeles to

culmination /kʌlmɪˈneɪʃən/ n.
the highest point or end of sth, usually happening after a long time
顶点,高潮

Washington, D.C, when I answered a lavatory call light in the coach cabin. There I found a young mother struggling with her **infant**. Everything was a mess, to say the least, and the mother, who was near **hysterics**, told me she had no more diapers or other clothing onboard the aircraft.

Through her tears, she informed me that they had missed their flight the previous night in Los Angeles and because she had very little money, she and her son had spent the night on the airport floor. Since she hadn't expected to miss the flight, she was forced to use up most of her supplies and whatever money she had to feed them.

5 With the saddest eyes I have ever seen she continued. She told me she was on her way to New Hampshire to deliver her son to the family that was **adopting** him. She could no longer support the two of them.

6 As she stood in front of me, crying, holding her beautiful son, I could see the **despair** and hopelessness on her face. And, as a mother of three beautiful daughters, I could feel her pain.

7 I immediately rang the flight attendant call button and asked for assistance from the other flight attendants. They brought cloth towels from first class to **assist** in cleaning up both mom and the infant. I ran and got my suitcase; because this woman and I were about the same size, I gave her a **sweater** and a pair of pants I had brought for my **layover**. Then I asked several families if they could spare extra diapers, **formula** and clothes for the child. After the young mother and her son had changed their clothes and the baby had gone to sleep, I sat with her, holding her hand, trying to provide some support and

---

infant /'infənt/ *n.*
child during the first few years of life
婴儿,幼儿

hysterics /hi'steriks/ *n.*
wild uncontrollable emotion
歇斯底里

adopt /ə'dɔpt/ *v.*
take sb into one's family as one's child
收养

despair /dis'pɛə/ *n.*
state of having lost all hope
绝望

assist /ə'sist/ *v.*
help
帮助,协助

sweater /'swetə/ *n.*
close-fitting knitted garment without fastening
针织紧身套衫

layover /'leiəuvə/ *n.*
(US) short stop on a journey
旅途中的短期停留

formula /'fɔ:mjulə/ *n.*
(US) artificial powdered milk for babies
人造婴儿奶粉

comfort for the remainder of the flight.

8   Once we landed, I walked them to their next flight, which would take them to their final destination. I briefed the gate **agent** and the new flight attendant crew on the situation and asked them to give her special attention.

9   With tears in my eyes I gave her a **hug** and told her, "You have shown me the true meaning of courage and a mother's love. I will never forget you."

10   As she thanked me for all I had done she said softly, "You're not the flight attendant, you're a sky angel." Touching my flight attendant wings, she continued, "And those are your angel wings."

11   With those words she turned and walked away, her child in her arms, and boarded the plane for New Hampshire.

12   Though I am no longer a flight attendant, my "angel wings" are still on **prominent** display in my office. And each time I see them, I am reminded of that young woman, her infant son and the gift that she gave me on that special day—that we truly are all **spiritual** beings traveling in human form.

(576 words)

> **agent** /'eidʒənt/ n.
> person who acts for other people in business, politics
> 代理人,经纪人
>
> **hug** /hʌg/ n.
> strong clasp with the arms
> 紧紧的拥抱
>
> **prominent** /'prɔminənt/ a.
> easily seen; distinguished
> 显著的,杰出的
>
> **spiritual** /'spiritjuəl/ a.
> of the human spirit
> 精神的,心灵的

Useful Phrases

stand out	be easily seen; be noticeable	突出,显眼
struggle with	try to overcome difficulties	拼搏,奋斗
to say the least	without any exaggeration	不夸张地说
use (sth) up	use (until) no more is left	耗尽,用完
on one's way	in the process of going	在路上
be near (hysterics)	almost reach	几乎,差点儿
assist (sb) with sth/ assist (sb) in (doing) sth	help	帮助,协助
provide sth for sb/ provide sb with sth	supply sth to sb	供给,供应

for the remainder of	for the rest of	剩余部分
walk sb to...	cause sb to walk by accompanying	陪伴某人走向……
remind... of...	tell sb to do sth he may forget	提醒

Notes

1 Earning my wings was the culmination of a childhood dream that I had set for myself after my first plane ride at the age of five. 在我五岁第一次乘坐飞机后，戴上空勤服务人员的徽章就成为我孩童时最大的梦想。

earning my wings 是动名词短语做主语；that I had set for myself after my first plane ride at the age of five 是一个 that 引导的定语从句，修饰前面的先行词 the culmination of a childhood dream；另外，wing 在该文中是一个双关语，既指"翅膀，机翼"，又指代"飞行员或空勤人员所佩戴的徽章"。

2 As she stood in front of me, crying, holding her beautiful son, I could see the despair and hopelessness on her face. 她哭着抱着她那漂亮的孩子站在我的面前，显得非常绝望无助。

As she stood in front of me 是 as 引导的一个时间状语从句；crying 和 holding her beautiful son 是两个伴随状语。

3 And each time I see them, I am reminded of that young woman, her infant son and the gift that she gave me on that special day—that we truly are all spiritual beings traveling in human form. 每次看见它们，我就想起了那位年轻的母亲和她的孩子，还有那天她送给我的礼物——我们真的是飞行在尘世间的崇高灵魂。

the gift 后面接了两个 that 从句：that she gave me on that special day 是一个限制性定语从句直接修饰前面的先行词 the gift；that we truly are all spiritual beings traveling in human form 是一个同位语从句，和 the gift 处于同等位置，进一步补充说明 the gift 的具体含义。

 **Exercises**

Reading Aloud and Memorizing the Following

I. Read the following paragraph taken from the text until you learn it by heart.

Though I am no longer a flight attendant, my "angel wings" are still on prominent display in my office. And each time I see them, I am reminded of that young woman, her infant son and the gift that she gave me on that special day—that we truly are all spiritual beings traveling in human form.

Comprehension of the Text

II. Choose the best answer to each of the following questions according to the passage.

1. According to the passage, all the following reasons are true except _____
   Why did the writer choose flight attendant as her profession?
   A. She wanted to fulfill her childhood dream to earn the wings.
   B. She fell in love with the romance of airplanes and adventures.
   C. It is a respectable job.
   D. She wanted to help others.

2. What problems didn't the woman and her baby encounter?
   A. They had missed their flight the previous night in Los Angeles.
   B. She could not find any family to adopt her child.
   C. They had to spend the night on the airport floor because of very little money.
   D. She had no more diapers or other clothing onboard the aircraft.

3. The writer provided the woman and her baby with many things except _____.
   A. cloth towels
   B. a sweater and a pair of pants
   C. diapers, formula and clothes for the child
   D. some money and a plane ticket

4. The final destination of the woman and her baby is _____.

   A. New Hampshire

   B. Washington, D.C

   C. Los Angeles

   D. New York

5. The word "wing" in the sentence "my angel wings are still on prominent display in my office" means _____.

   A. either of the pair of feathered limbs that a bird uses to fly

   B. part that projects from the side of an aircraft and supports it in the air

   C. part of a political party that holds certain views

   D. pilot's badge

III. Answer the following questions with the information you've got from the text.

1. Why did the writer choose to become a flight attendant?   (Para. 1)
2. What did the writer find when she answered a lavatory call light in the coach cabin?   (Para. 3)
3. Why did the woman fly to New Hampshire?   (Para. 5)
4. How did the writer help the woman once they landed?   (Para. 8)
5. Why did the woman call the writer "sky angel"?   (Para. 12)

Vocabulary

IV. Find the definition in column B which matches the words or expressions in column A.

A	B
1. adventure	( ) a. be noticeable
2. supplies	( ) b. take to a place
3. feed	( ) c. help
4. deliver	( ) d. for the rest of
5. despair	( ) e. hopelessness
6. assist sb in doing	( ) f. outstanding

7. extra   ( ) g. give food to
8. prominent   ( ) h. exciting experience
9. stand out   ( ) i. things provided
10. for the remainder of   ( ) j. additional

V. **Fill in the blanks with the words given in the brackets. Change the form where necessary.**

1. Halloween is a _____ holiday for American children. (adventure)
2. There are many _____ fans at Cuijian's rock concert. (hysterics)
3. The prisoner grew more _____ when he was sent to the electric chair. (despair)
4. Please call if you require _____. (assist)
5. He got a job from an employment _____. (agent)
6. She gave her mother an affectionate _____. (hug)
7. This ordinary-looking man is an officer of _____ in public life. (prominent)
8. They are _____ to meet and get married. (destination)
9. The _____ of his suggestion is a wise decision. (adopt)
10. Although they lost, the team played with great _____. (spiritual)

VI. **Complete each of the following sentences with the most appropriate word or words from the four choices marked A, B, C and D.**

1. Her work stand _____ from the others in the company
   A. on   B. for   C. away   D. out
2. The passengers were forced to jump into the sea from the sinking ship and struggled _____ the coldness helplessly.
   A. to   B. with   C. for   D. in
3. Please remind me _____ I should post the letter this morning.
   A. of   B. to   C. that   D. which
4. The teacher provided his students _____ many books.
   A. for   B. with   C. of   D. at
5. Fossil fuels are going to be used _____ in 100 years.
   A. of   B. up   C. out   D. from
6. We are satisfied with the successful _____ of the long struggle.
   A. plan   B. thought   C. campaign   D. culmination

7. A lot of volunteers went to Wenchuan County to assist the victims in the earthquake _____ great passion and responsibility.

   A. in   B. with   C. for   D. of

8. Could you _____ me a few minutes? I know you are busy but I really want to talk to you.

   A. give   B. save   C. spare   D. make

9. The American couple _____ the 5-year-old Chinese girl.

   A. raised   B. fed   C. adopted   D. delivered

10. There is a film _____ tonight directed by Chen Kaige.

    A. on   B. off   C. show   D. showing

Structure

VII. Rewrite the following sentences after the models.

Model 1   They brought cloth towels from first class to help clean up both mom and the infant.

> They brought cloth towels from first class to **assist in cleaning up** both mom and the infant.

1. The secretary helped the manager with many of his duties.
2. The man was cooperating with the police in answering their questions.
3. You are required to help Mr. Smith prepare this report.
4. The luggage is heavy. Will you help me carry them upstairs?
5. Please do me a favor to check up the result of my experiment.

Model 2   And each time I see them, I remembered that young woman.

> And each time I see them, I **am reminded of** that young woman.

1. Do I have to inform you of his arrival again?
2. The clock made me remember I must feed the cat now.
3. Please tell me when to answer the call.
4. This English song made me think of my school year.
5. Travelers are informed that they should pay the tickets themselves.

VIII. Study the model and translate the following sentences into English.

Model   **With tears in my eyes**, I gave her a hug and told her.

1. 老师手臂下夹着书，走进了教室。
2. 海伦脸上挂着微笑，向我点了点头。
3. 母亲双臂紧紧抱着我，哭了起来。
4. 他桌上的书堆得太多，只好放一些书到书橱里。
5. 由于他作文里都是拼写错误，老师很生气。

IX. Translate the following sentences into Chinese.

1. I have flown hundreds of flights since graduation, but one stands out among the many.

2. There I found a young mother struggling with her infant.

3. As she stood in front of me, crying, holding her beautiful son, I could see the despair and hopelessness on her face.

4. Once we landed, I walked them to their next flight, which would take them to their final destination.

5. Though I am no longer a flight attendant, my "angel wings" are still on prominent display in my office.

X. Translate the following sentences into English using the words or phrases in the brackets.

1. 她寝室的同学都很优秀，而她则是最突出的一个。(stand out)

2. 由于汽车的汽油用完了，他们只有步行回家了。(use up)

3. 虽然他的英语很差，但他很努力学习并取得了很大进步。(struggle with)

4. 这个公司给它的职员提供了很多机会来提升自己。(provide)

5. 请提醒我明天早上早点儿起床。(remind)

Part II Grammar

Types of Sentences（句子类型）

句子按其结构可分为简单句、并列句、复合句三种类型

1. 简单句(Simple Sentence)，只包含一个独立分句的句子。简单句内只有一套主语和谓语结构，其中可以有并列的主语，也可以有并列的谓语动词。简单句有主语+谓语(+状语)、主语+连系动词+表语、主语+谓语+宾语、主语+谓语+宾语+补语和主语+谓语+间接宾语和直接宾语或+双宾语五种基本结构。

Examples:

Everybody knows.	每个人都知道。
I looked at the man and the woman angrily.	我气愤地看着这对男女。
She looks very beautiful.	她看起来很漂亮。
He is reading a book in the library.	他正在图书馆读书。
I consider him my best friend.	我把他看成我最好的朋友。
I'll read you the letter.	我会给你读这封信。
He asked me a question.	他问了我一个问题。

2. 并列句(Compound Sentence)，有两个或两个以上的简单句(即分句)组成，常见的并列句结构是：简单句+连接词+简单句。这种简单句常被叫做分句。并列连接词有：and, but, so, yet, or, as well as, both ... and..., either... or..., neither ... nor..., not only ... but also ..., then, however, therefore, nevertheless, still, for。并列连接词可表示添加、选择、转折或对比、因果等意义。

Examples:

It's not cheap, but it's very good.	这东西是不便宜，但却很好。
This is me and these are my friends.	这是我，这些是我的朋友。
The fish must stay in water, or they will die.	鱼类必须呆在水里，否则就会死去。
I will not do that, for it would be of no use.	我不愿做那事，因为不会有什么益处。

She was very tired, nevertheless she kept on working.

　　　　　　　　　　　　　　她很累了，但仍坚持工作。

　　3. 复合句(Complex Sentence)，由一个主句和一个或一个以上的从句组成。主句是全句的主体，通常可以独立存在；从句则是一个句子成分，不能独立存在。复合句可分为并列复合句和主从复合句。主从复合句中的从句有定语从句、状语从句、名词性从句(主语从句、宾语从句、表语从句和同位语从句)之分。引导从句的关联词有：if, because, although, as, that, who, which, whom, what, whose, when, where, why, how, whatever, whoever, whichever, whether。

Examples:

　　It is doubtful whether he is coming.　他是否来尚不确定。
　　That is what I mean.　　　　　　　这就是我的意思。
　　He said that he didn't like you.　　　他说他不喜欢你。
　　Everybody believes the truth that the earth moves around the sun.

　　　　　　　　　　　　　　人人都相信地球围着太阳转这一真理。

　　The man who is talking with the teacher is my father.

　　　　　　　　　　　　　　正和老师谈话的那个人是我父亲。

　　When you cross a main road, you must be careful.

　　　　　　　　　　　　　　你穿过大街时可要小心。

I. Complete each of the following sentences with the most appropriate word or words from the four choices marked A, B, C and D.

1. Things got _____ bad recently _____ he decided to go on a diet.
　A. such ... that　　B. such ... which　C. so ... that　　D. so ... which

2. Not only the mother _____ the children were ill.
　A. and　　　　　　B. but also　　　　C. or　　　　　　D. nor

3. There was no one there, _____ we went away.
　A. and　　　　　　B. or　　　　　　　C. so　　　　　　D. but

4. It is not known _____ he is.
　A. that　　　　　　B. why　　　　　　C. who　　　　　　D. whose

5. You should act on _____ the teacher told you.
   A. what   B. that   C. whether   D. how
6. The teacher gave us the suggestion _____ we should learn English well.
   A. what   B. when   C. that   D. why
7. The problem is _____ we can get to replace her.
   A. that   B. who   C. what   D. why
8. Have you set the day _____ you will move?
   A. where   B. that   C. why   D. when
9. There are still many people _____ living conditions are miserable.
   A. that   B. whose   C. which   D. who
10. The book is on the table ___ you left it.
   A. which   B. where   C. why   D. that

II. Tell what kind of sentence the following sentences are.

1. A young man and a young woman were sitting behind me and talking loudly.
2. I bought the book in the bookstore last Sunday.
3. Would you like coffee, milk or tea?
4. He worked hard, but failed.
5. I was late for school because I overslept.
6. It is said that he has got married.
7. Don't leave until I've spoken to you.
8. A doctor is a person who looks after people's health.

III. Fill in the blanks with the words given in the box in their proper forms.

| but | or | for | and | until | whether | although | so that |

1. _____ he comes to the party or not is none of my business.
2. I want to become a teacher, _____ it is a respectable job.
3. Turn around the corner, _____ you will see the post office.
4. _____ he is wealthy, he is quite modest and easygoing.
5. Turn on the tap _____ the hot water flows out.
6. To be _____ not to be, this is a question.
7. I'd like to go with you, _____ I have to finish the paper first.
8. Go on pursuing your dream _____ you will be successful in the near future.

Part III Reading Practice

Guide to Reading

1. Words and Expressions to Learn

companion	n.	伙伴,同伴
faithful	adj.	忠实的
tug	v.	用力拖或拉某事物
breeze	n.	微风
hurricane	n.	飓风
toss	v.	抛
Puerto Rico		波多黎各(拉丁美洲一岛国)
be devoted to		忠实于,专心于,奉献于
pull out		离开,拉出
make a / no / some / much difference to sth / sb		对某人/某事物有/没有/有些……作用或影响
give a thought to		考虑到,想到

2. Pre-Reading Questions

(1) Have you ever raised any pets? If yes, please share your experience with your classmates?

(2) What do you think are the characteristics of dogs, cats or other pets?

The Stone Dog

1 Long, long ago, there lived a poor fisherman, alone in a house and his only companion was his dog. The fisherman and his dog were devoted to each other.

They might be seen walking on the white sandy beach, or coming through the bushes. However, there was one place where nobody saw them together. That was in the fisherman's boat.

2   But the dog was always beside his master as the fisherman made his little boat ready to sail. When the man pulled out to sea each morning, the dog would ran up on the high **ridge** (*n.* 山脊), where he would sit and watch all day. The dog never moved until late afternoon when he saw the little boat return. Then he would race back to the shore to greet his master. And together the man and the dog would set off for the town to sell the fresh-caught fish.

3   As the years went by, the fisherman grew older. So did the faithful dog. The fisherman still went out to sea. The dog still watched for his return, sitting on the high ridge.

4   One morning early in September, the fisherman was getting his little boat ready. All at once the dog began to bark and **howl** (*v.* 嚎叫). He circled around the fisherman and tugged at his trousers. The fisherman could not remember when he had seen his dog act so strangely. He patted the dog's back, thinking the dog wanted to play, but nothing made any difference. The dog kept barking. The fisherman laughed and continued getting ready. Then he climbed into the boat and sailed away. The dog went to his watching place, still barking and howling.

5   There were other fishing boats out that morning. The sky was blue and the breeze soft and fresh. Suddenly the soft breeze changed. It began to blow wildly. The fisherman's boat was seized by the wind and **whirled** (*v.* 打转) around. The sky darkened and rain began to fall.

6   "It's a hurricane!" said the fisherman. The man thought of his dog at once. Had the dog left the ridge and run home or was he still sitting there? The fisherman tried to **steer** (*v.* 操纵) his boat and turn it toward the shore. Suddenly a great wave swept over his head and tossed the boat away.

7   When dawn came next morning,

the hurricane was over. The sky was blue once more. When the sun rose over the mountains, the families of the other fishermen ran to the shore. They watched for the return of the boats. They waited and waited, but no one returned. Then the people went slowly back to their homes, but none of them gave a thought to the fisherman's dog.

8   Several months later a group of villagers noticed what appeared to be the figure of a dog sitting high on the ridge.

9   "Look," said one. " Isn't that the old fisherman's dog?"

10   " How could it be, after all this time?" said another.

11   To prove his point, the first man climbed the stony ridge to get hold of the dog. But when he reached the spot, he only found a rock—a rock shaped like a dog. The man came down quickly. But as soon as the people looked up again, they saw the stone dog. His head was held high. He just sat there on top of the ridge, waiting, waiting...

(600 words)

Reading Comprehension

I. Answer the following questions according to the passage.

1. How were the fisherman and his dog devoted to each other?

2. What would the dog do when the fisherman pulled out to sea every morning?

3. What messages did the dog want to convey to his master through his barking one morning?

4. Can you guess what happened to the fisherman in the hurricane?

5. Was the dog finally turned into a stone? Use your imagination to make up a short story about what happened to the dog after the hurricane?

II. Translate into Chinese the following sentences taken from the passage.

1. The dog was always beside his master as the fisherman made his little boat ready to sail.
2. The dog never moved until late afternoon when he saw the little boat return.
3. The fisherman could not remember when he had seen his dog act so strangely.
4. Then the people went slowly back to their homes, but none of them gave a thought to the fisherman's dog.
5. Several months later a group of villagers noticed what appeared to be the figure of a dog sitting high on the ridge.

III. Fill in the blanks with the words or phrases listed in Words and Expressions to Learn. Change the form where necessary.

1. A dog is an honest _____ for the old man.
2. She was always _____ to her husband.
3. The man is _____ to science.
4. I arrived as the last train _____ off the station.
5. It won't _____ whether you go today or tomorrow.
6. She would never _____ marrying someone so old.
7. In spring, we often enjoy the _____ that comes from the lake.
8. The young man in jeans _____ a coin to the beggar.

IV. Complete the following sentences.

1. The plane _____ (撞了桥), killing most of the passengers and the crew.
2. You will be fined if you don't _____ (系牢安全带) while driving.
3. The police _____ (调查这起案件) and then arrested the suspect.
4. Whether he accept the offer or not _____ (对我来说没任何分别).
5. He _____ (后悔在考试中舞弊), but it is too late.
6. To encourage home consumption, we have _____ (降息) three times in the past year.
7. The soldiers were ready to _____ (挑战死亡) to rescue as many survivors as possible.
8. The American president _____ (做了漂亮的演说) at the ceremony.

Part IV Practical English

Notes（便条）

便条是一种简单的书信形式，内容简短，文字紧凑，称呼格式化，大多是临时性的留言，一般不写地址。内容有询问、请示、通知、要求等。

1. Asking for leave（请假条）

请假条有事假条、病假条等。请假条是由个人向组织提交的，因此文体应正规，内容须紧凑，理由要充分，必要时，应附上证明。

如：

> Dear Mr. Pike,
>
>   I very much regret I was unable to attend school this morning owing to a severe attack of illness. I am enclosing here with a certificate from the doctor who is attending me, as he fears it will be several days before I shall be able to resume my study. I trust my enforced absence will not give you any serious inconvenience.
>
>   Sincerely yours,
>
>   Jack

亲爱的派克先生：

    非常抱歉，我因今晨突然生病不能前来上课。现附上医生证明，医生担心我也许要几天后才能上课。希望我这次身不由己的缺勤不致给您带来很大的麻烦。

您诚挚的

杰克

2. Message Left（留言条）

可用于说明一件事、做一次活动安排以及询问等等，应直截了当。写留言条，日期部分写在右上角，一般只写星期几，或星期几上午、下午或具体钟点。

如：

8:30 A. M.

Dear Peter:

    I have done all my things here. I sincerely thank you for the trouble you have taken for my sake. I am leaving for home by train at two this afternoon. This is to say good-bye to you. Please remember me to your wife.

Yours ever,

Jack

亲爱的彼得：

    我在这里的事情已经全部办好。这次麻烦你了，我万分感激。我定于今天下午两点乘火车返家，特来辞行，并请代向你的妻子问好。

挚友 杰克

上午 8 时 30 分

Useful Expressions

Encl.: Doctor's Certificate of Advice.
Yours note with an admission ticket enclosed is much appreciated.
Please give an extension of leave for three days.
I shall feel obliged if you will favor me with a call at your earliest convenience.
Will call at 2 p.m. tomorrow.

附：医生证明
留言和一张入场券均已收到，不胜感激。
请准予续假三天为盼。
如您方便，请早日来电，我将不胜感激。
定于明天下午两点拜访。

Exercises

1. Fill in the blanks in the following English note so that it is functionally equivalent to the Chinese version.

老师：
　　由于重感冒，我今天不能来上课，有医生开具的证明为据。
　　希望您能原谅我的缺席。

　　　　　　　　　　　　　您真诚的
　　　　　　　　　　　　　乔治·泰勒

Dear Sir,
　　_____ a bad cold, I _____ attend classes today. I now submit a _____ issued by the doctor.
　　Hoping you will excuse my non-attendance.

　　　　　　　　　　　　　Yours sincerely,
　　　　　　　　　　　　　George Tailor

2. Write a telephone message to tell Mr. Charles that Anna phoned that she would leave for New York tomorrow afternoon, and asked him to call back.

Part V English Salon

English Poem

Life
by Langston Hughes

Life can be good,
Life can be bad;
Life is mostly cheerful,
But sometimes sad.

Life can be dreams,
Life can be great thoughts;
Life can mean a person,
Sitting in court.

Life can be dirty,
Life can even be painful;
But life is what you make it,
So try to make it beautiful.

Read aloud the poem and then recite it.

Unit Four

Part I Text

Guide to Text-Learning

1. Theme of the Text

    Darwin is the first of the evolutionary biologists, the originator of the concept of natural selection. His principal works, *The Origin of Species by Means of Natural Selection* (1859) and *The Descent of Man* (1871) marked a new epoch. His works were violently attacked and energetically defended, then; and, it seems, yet today.

2. Words and Expressions Related to the Topic

variation	变异,变种
origin	起源,起因
species	种类
evolution	演变,进化
naturalist	自然学家;自然主义者
specialization	特殊化;专门化;特化作用
race	种族;种族特征
botany	植物学
Charles Robert Darwin	查尔斯·罗伯特·达尔文
natural selection	自然选择

3. Grammatical Structure to Learn

    (1) On the Galapagos Islands in the Pacific Ocean he noticed many variations among plants and animals of **the same** general type **as** those in South America.

在太平洋的加拉帕戈斯群岛上，他注意到岛上那些跟南美的动植物同属一般物种的动植物所衍生的许多变异。

(2) Darwin was a reserved, thorough, hard working scholar who concerned himself with the feelings and emotions **not only** of his family, **but** of his friends and peers **as well.**

达尔文是一个稳重、执着而又勤奋的学者。不论是对亲朋好友还是同行，他都十分在乎他们的想法与情感。

(3) **It has been supposed** that Darwin renounced evolution on his deathbed.

人们一直认为，达尔文临终前宣布放弃了他的进化论。

4. Grammar

Basic Sentence Patterns I: 1. SV（主语＋不及物动词）；2. SVP（主语＋连系动词＋表语）；3. There be 存在句型。

5. Practical English

I.O.U. and Receipt Forms

Warm-Up Questions:

1. What is Charles Darwin?
2. What are the related theories out of Darwin's study when he returned to London?
3. What are people's attitudes towards Darwin's theory?

1　　I have called this **principle**, by which each slight variation, if useful, is preserved, by the term Natural Selection.

—From *The Origin of Species* by Charles Darwin

principle /ˈprinsəpl/ *n.*
a basic truth, law, or assumption
原则

2

Charles Robert Darwin was born on February 12, 1809 in Shrewsbury, England. He was the fifth child and second son of Robert Waring Darwin and Susannah Wedgwood. Darwin was the British naturalist who became famous for his theories of evolution and natural **selection**. Like several scientists before him, Darwin believed all the life on earth **evolved** (developed gradually) over millions of years from a few common **ancestors**.

3

From 1831 to 1836 Darwin served as naturalist aboard the H.M.S. Beagle on a British science expedition around the world. In South America Darwin found fossils of extinct animals that were similar to modern **species**. On the Galapagos Islands in the Pacific Ocean he noticed many **variations** among plants and animals of the same general type as those in South America. The expedition visited places around the world, and Darwin studied plants and animals everywhere he went, collecting specimens for further study.

4

Upon his return to London Darwin conducted thorough research of his notes and specimens. Out of this study grew several related theories: one, **evolution** did **occur**; two, evolutionary change was gradual, requiring thousands to millions of years; three, the primary **mechanism** for evolution was a process called natural selection; and four, the millions of species alive today arose from a single original life form through a branching process called specialization.

---

selection /si'lekʃən/ n.
act of selecting
选择，挑选

evolve /i'vɔlv/ v.
develop gradually
进化；发展

ancestor /'ænsestə/ n.
a person in your family who lived a long time before you, from whom you are descended
祖先，祖宗

species /'spi:ʃiz/ n.
a group of plants or animals that are similar to each other
种类

variation /ˌvɛəri'eiʃən/ n.
a difference in quality or quantity befween a lot of things
进化，变异

evolution /ˌi:və'lu:ʃən, ˌevə-/ n.
the development of living things over many years from simple early forms
进化

occur /ə'kəː/ v.
take place; come about
发生；出现

mechanism /'mekənizəm/ n.
the way that sth works
机制；机构

5   Darwin's theory of evolutionary selection holds that variation within species occurs randomly and that the **survival** or extinction of each organism is determined by that organism's ability to adapt to its environment. He set these theories forth in his book called, *On the Origin of Species by Means of Natural Selection,* or *The Preservation of Favoured Races in the Struggle for Life* (1859) or *The Origin of Species* for short. After publication of *The Origin of Species,* Darwin continued to write on botany, geology, and zoology until his death in 1882. He is buried in Westminster Abbey.

6   Darwin's work had a **tremendous impact** on **religious** thought. Many people strongly **opposed** the idea of evolution because it conflicted with their religious **convictions**. Darwin avoided talking about the theological and sociological aspects of his work, but other writers used his theories to support their own theories about society. Darwin was a reserved, thorough, hard working scholar who concerned himself with the feelings and emotions not only of his family, but of his friends and peers as well.

7   It has been supposed that Darwin **renounced** evolution on his deathbed. Shortly after his death, temperance campaigner and **evangelist** Lady Elizabeth Hope claimed she visited Darwin at his deathbed, and witnessed the renunciation. Her story was printed in a Boston newspaper and **subsequently** spread. Lady Hope's story was **refuted** by Darwin's daughter Henrietta who stated, "I was present at his deathbed ... He never recanted any of his scientific views, either then or earlier."

(498 words)

---

survival /sə'vaivəl/ *n.*
the state of continuing to live or exist
生存,幸存

tremendous /tri'mendəs/ *adj.*
enormous
强烈地;极大的

impact /'impækt/ *n.*
the effect or impression of one thing on another
冲击,影响

religious /ri'lidʒəs/ *adj.*
connected with religion
信奉宗教的,虔诚的

oppose /ə'pəuz/ *v.*
disagree with sth
反对,抗争

conviction /kən'vikʃən/ *n.*
a fixed or strong belief
信条,信念

renounce /ri'nauns/ *v.*
reject; give up
否认;放弃

evangelist /i'vændʒilist/ *n.*
one who practices evangelism
福音传道者

subsequently /'sʌbsikwəntli/ *ad.*
after an event in the past
后来,随后

refute /ri'fju:t/ *v.*
deny
驳斥;否认

Useful Phrases

on expedition	a journey undertaken by a group of people	考察；旅行
be similar to	almost the same	相似的，类似的
the same ... as	in the same way	与……同样的
adapt to	get used to a new situation	适应
set forth	write or talk about an idea or an argument	阐明；提出
conflict with	cannot exist together	冲突，斗争
concern with	love or care about someone	关心，爱护
it is supposed	be believed to be sth by many people	人们认为

Proper Names

British Naturalist 1809—1882 Charles Robert Darwin	查尔斯·罗伯特·达尔文
The Origin of Species	《物种起源》
Shrewsbury	什鲁斯伯里
Susannah Wedgwood	苏珊娜·韦奇伍德
the H.M.S. Beagle	猎犬号（船）
the Galapagos Islands	加拉帕戈斯群岛
Westminster Abbey	威斯敏斯特教堂（亦称"西敏寺"）

Notes

1. Like several scientists before him, Darwin believed all the life on earth evolved (developed gradually) over millions of years from a few common ancestors. 像他之前的几位科学家一样，达尔文认为地球上所有的生

命都是经由少数几个共同的祖先，经过千百万年的进化(逐渐的发展)演变而来的。

like 这里作介词,意为"像……一样"; millions of (years)表示"数以百万计的",可以翻译为"成百上千万(年)"。类似的用法还有 hundreds of..., thousands of...等等; evolve from 表示"由……演变而来"。

2. Out of this study grew several related theories... 由此产生了好几个相关的理论。

这是一个全部倒装句。此句可还原为 Several related theories grew out of this study.

3. Many people strongly opposed the idea of evolution because it conflicted with their religious convictions. 由于进化论的观点与人们的宗教信条相冲突,从而招致许多人的极力反对。

4. I was present at his deathbed ... He never recanted any of his scientific views, either then or earlier. 父亲临终前我也在场……无论是在当时或是在以前,他从未放弃过他的任何科学主张。

be present 指某人在现场, present 在这里作形容词用,它也可以作名词表示"礼物"。第二句中的 either...or...表示"两者中的任何一个"。若是两者都不,则用短语 neither...nor...

Reading Aloud and Memorizing the Following

I. Read the following paragraph taken from the text until you learn it by heart.

Upon his return to London Darwin conducted thorough research of his notes and specimens. Out of this study grew several related theories: one, evolution did occur; two, evolutionary change was gradual, requiring thousands to millions of years; three, the primary mechanism for evolution was a process called natural

selection; and four, the millions of species alive today arose from a single original life form through a branching process called specialization.

Comprehension of the text

II. Choose the best answer to each of the following questions according to the passage.

1. According to the passage, Darwin became famous for _____.
   A. science expedition around the world
   B. theory of evolution and natural selection
   C. Natural Selection
   D. the tremendous impact of his theory on religious thought

2. Where did Darwin find the fossils of extinct animals?
   A. Galapagos Islands in the Pacific Ocean.   B. Shrewsbury, England.
   C. London.   D. South America.

3. Which statement is true according to the passage?
   A. There are three related theories out of Darwin's study.
   B. The survival and extinction of each organism is not determined by its ability to adapt to its environment.
   C. Darwin's theories of evolutionary selection come from his book called *The Origin of Species*.
   D. Darwin renounced evolution on his deathbed.

4. What kind of person is Darwin?
   A. He is concerned with himself.
   B. He is a workaholic.
   C. He is a hardworking scholar who cares for others.
   D. He is a professor with a strong belief in religion.

5. What did Lady Elizabeth Hope claim?
   A. She claimed that Darwin never renounced his theory.
   B. She claimed that he renounced his scientific views at an early time.
   C. She claimed that she witnessed Darwin's renunciation of his theory of evolution.
   D. She claimed that she visited Darwin and his daughter Henrietta.

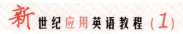

III. Answer the following questions with the information you've got from the text.

1. What did Darwin do from 1831 to 1836? (Para. 2)
2. What is the third related theory out of his study which was conducted when he returned to London? (Para. 4)
3. What determines the survival and extinction of each organism? (Para. 5)
4. Why did many people strongly oppose Darwin's idea of evolution? (Para. 6)
5. How did Darwin's daughter respond to Lady Elizabeth Hope's claim? (Para. 7)

Vocabulary

IV. Find the definition in column B which matches the words or expressions in column A.

A	B
1. principle	( ) a. develop
2. evolve	( ) b. forebear
3. occur	( ) c. alive
4. ancestor	( ) d. accommodate
5. survival	( ) e. deny
6. adapt to	( ) f. be against
7. tremendous	( ) g. opposition
8. conflict with	( ) h. enormous
9. oppose	( ) i. happen
10. refute	( ) j. rule

V. Fill in the blanks with the words given in the brackets. Change the form where necessary.

1. He was _____ to represent the school to take part into the English competition. (select)
2. They hold a strong _____ in Christianity. (believe)
3. An afternoon tea _____ to all our guests. (serve)

4. The _____ between the sisters can easily be seen. (similar)
5. _____ speaking, boys like football more than girls. (general)
6. Scientists have been _____ on effects of the drug on mice. (research)
7. He was lucky enough to _____ the plane crash. (survival)
8. The movie _____ from this novel was very successful. (adapt)
9. Lady Elizabeth Hope said that she witnessed the _____. (renounce)
10. The new fossil may tell us more about human _____. (evolve)

VI. Complete each of the following sentences with the most appropriate word or words from the four choices marked A, B, C and D.

1. Venice is famous _____ its beautiful scenery.
   A. of   B. in   C. for   D. from
2. He is _____ his father very much.
   A. liking   B. as   C. like   D. looking
3. They received _____ of letters asking for information.
   A. million   B. three millions   C. millions   D. many million
4. Something interesting arose _____ the meeting.
   A. in   B. from   C. of   D. out
5. Bird Flu has a great impact _____ the whole world.
   A. in   B. up   C. on   D. over
6. _____ is a study that deals with animal and animal life.
   A. Botany   B. Geology   C. Zoology   D. Psychology
7. He had to brake hard in order to avoid _____ that little boy.
   A. hit   B. to   C. from hitting   D. hitting
8. She is _____ conflict _____ her boss.
   A. in, with   B. over, between   C. in, between   D. over, with
9. Ross is never _____ about what other people think of him.
   A. concerned   B. worried   C. cared   D. anxious
10. He is a _____ to the accident.
    A. people   B. witness   C. human   D. fellow

Structure

VII. Rewrite the following sentences after the models.

Model 1 He likes both his parents and his friends.

He likes **not only** his parents, **but also** his friends.

1. She said that she would go to the USA and Singapore as well.
2. I would go to visit my teacher and my former classmates, too.
3. I don't care what his attitude is and how he will respond to the criticism.
4. Shakespeare is a writer and an actor.
5. Oscar likes both English and French.

Model 2 People thought that he won the lottery.

It's supposed that he won the lottery.

1. They suppose that it will rain tomorrow.
2. Scientists thought that large dinosaurs lived in swamps.
3. All my friends think that we are going to sell that house.
4. All my classmates think language is complex.
5. They think that waste is a kind of crime.

VIII. Study the model and translate the following sentences into English.

Model He looks **the same as** his farther.

1. 同学们和老师做的一样。
2. 他和我喜欢一样的食物。
3. 今天的天气和昨天一样好。
4. 实验若想要成功,就一定要按照要求做。
5. rain 和 reign 的发音是一样的。

Translation

IX. Translate the following sentences into Chinese.

1. Darwin was the British naturalist who became famous for his theories of evolution

and natural selection.

2. The expedition visited places around the world, and Darwin studied plants and animals everywhere he went, collecting specimens for further study.

3. Upon his return to London Darwin conducted thorough research of his notes and specimens.

4. The survival or extinction of each organism is determined by that organism's ability to adapt to its environment.

5. It has been supposed that Darwin renounced evolution on his deathbed.

X. Translate the following sentences into English using the words or phrases in the brackets.

1. 我的观点和老师的很相似。(be similar to)

2. 学生很快适应了新的学校。(adapt to)

3. 目击者的陈述和警察的证据相左。(conflict with)

4. 所有人都很关心儿童的教育。(be concerned with)

5. 布朗正带领他的团队进行对南极的科学考察。(on expedition)

Part II Grammar

Basic Sentence Patterns（基本句型）I

1. **SV**（主语+不及物动词）

　　SV 结构是英语核心结构，其他的结构都是以此为基础变化而来的。其中，动词为不及物动词，因此后面不能接宾语，也没有被动语态的形式，但可以跟状语。SV 中的不及物动词说明主语所发出的动作或存在的状态，句中所出现的状语一般限制谓语。

Examples：

　　The flowers are blooming.

　　She works very hard.

　　She comes from China.

　　They arrived in Beijing yesterday evening.

2. **SVP**（主语+连系动词 + 表语）

　　SVP 结构最常出现的动词是连系动词，其中 be 动词最常见。其余常见的还有 look, feel, smell, sound, taste, seem, appear, become, get, grow, turn , remain, keep 等。表语可以由名词、形容词、介词短语等充当。

Examples:

　　Miss Jones is a teacher.

　　The flower looks beautiful.

　　He is from Beijing.

　　SVP 结构还有一种被称为"双谓语"的情况，通常由"主语 + 实义动词 + 形容词(过去分词)"构成。例如：

　　The sun rises red. (=The sun is red when it rises.)

　　He died young. (= He died when he was young.)

3. **There be** 存在句型。该句型通常以非重读 there 为形式主语，以动词 be 或其他含有"存在"意义的动词的一定形式作谓语，其常见结构通常为：

　　(1) There + be + N + Ad.

　　There are many places of interest in China.

There are twelve months in a year.

(2) **There + be + N + Attrib.**

There is something wrong with my watch.

There isn't any shop open after 9 p.m. here.

(3) **There + V + N + Ad.**

There stands a tall tree in the yard.

There exists no life on the moon.

There seems to be a berry pie cooking in the kitchen.

I. Point out the patterns of the following sentences and then translate them into Chinese.

1. She is running.

2. There are many students on campus.

3. He left unhappily.

4. The traffic lights turn red and all the cars stop.

5. Every minute counts.

6. That hamburger tastes delicious.

7. There lays a basket of apples on the table.

8. There is no one interested in computer games in our class.

II. Filling the blanks with proper words according to the requirements.

1. There _____ a beautiful princess a long time ago. (There + V + N + Ad.)
2. In spring, all trees _____ green. (SVP)
3. This job _____ easy. (SVP)
4. The moon _____ in the evening. (SV)
5. There _____ a table, two desks and three lights in this room.
   (There + be + N + Ad.)

III. Fill in the blanks with the words given in the box in their proper forms.

| silence | die | old | sweets | slow |
| terribly | excite | happily | interest | cold |

1. He always keeps _____ at the meeting.
2. She looks _____ today.
3. It's getting _____ and _____.
4. This flower smells very _____.
5. The fish tastes very _____.
6. He became _____ after hearing the news.
7. His father _____ two years ago.
8. Your plan sounds _____.
9. Plants grow very _____ in winter.
10. She's growing _____.

Part III   Reading Practice

Guide to Reading

1. Words and Expressions to Learn

worldwide	*adj.*	全世界的
volunteer	*n.*	自愿者
financial	*adj.*	金钱的,财政的
darken	*v.*	黯淡,(使)变暗
satirist	*n.*	讽刺作家,爱说挖苦话的人
portion	*n.*	一部分,一份
triumph	*n.& v.*	成功,胜利
ban	*v.*	禁止
work as		以……身份工作
relate... to		与……相关
meet with		遭遇,遭受
Mark Twain		马克·吐温
Samuel Langhorne Clemens		塞缪尔·朗霍恩·克莱门斯
Florida, Missouri		密苏里州佛罗里达
Territorial Enterprise		《事业报》
Charles Dudley Warner		查尔斯·杜德利·华纳
Olivia Langdon		奥莉维亚·朗顿

2. Pre-Reading Questions:

(1) Do you know Mark Twain?

(2) What do you think about him?

Mark Twain

1   Mark Twain, whose real name was Samuel Langhorne Clemens when he was born on November 30,1835 in Florida, Missouri, of a Virginian family, was an American writer, journalist and humorist. He won a worldwide audience for his stories of the youthful adventures of Tom Sawyer and Huckleberry Finn.

2   After his father's death in 1847, he led many different lives. He lived and worked all over the world, he was **apprenticed** (*v.* 当学徒) to a printer and wrote for his brother's newspaper. He later worked as a Mississippi river-boat pilot. The Civil War put an end to the steamboat traffic and Clemens moved to Virginia City to volunteer in the war on the side of Union, where he edited the *Territorial Enterprise*. On February 3, 1863, "Mark Twain" was born when Clemens signed a humorous travel account with that **pseudonym** (*n.* 笔名).

3   Twain left for California in 1864, and worked as a reporter in San Francisco. The work that first brought Twain literary acclaim was *Jim Smiley and His Jumping Frog* in 1865. The success as a writer gave Twain enough financial security to marry Olivia Langdon in 1870. They moved next year to Hartford. Twain continued to lecture in the United States and England. Between 1876 and 1884, he published several masterpieces, *Tom Sawyer* (1881) and *The Prince and the Pauper* (1881), *Life on the Mississippi* appeared in 1883 and *Huckleberry Finn* in 1884.

4   With his long and rich life, Twain wrote about his many experiences. Even when there's obvious bitterness related to some of his experiences, he put in the narrative with humor; even in tragedy, he's able to triumph through the power of language. The death of his wife and his second daughter darkened

Twain's later years, which is seen in his **autobiography** (*n.* 自传) published after his death. We can hear him crying out in words after their deaths. As his writing about that, so it becomes clear that not enough could ever be written about his life. The spirits of the dead seem to surround him, **weighing him down**(使他消沉).

5   Mark Twain died on April 21, 1910. He has been called a realist and a romantic, a humorist and a satirist. His mark on American literary history cannot be **overstated** (*v.* 夸大叙述). The popularity of his works has been met with an equal portion of argument, with *Huckleberry Finn* as one of the most **banned** (*v.* 禁止) and **debated** (*v.* 争议) books in American literature. His life was remarkable in its triumphs and tragedies. His words are remarkable in their depth and insight of human experience.

Reading Comprehension

I. Answer the following questions according to the passage.

1. What works helped Mark Twain win a world wide audience?
2. When was the pseudonym used for the first time?
3. Which work first won Mark Twain literary fame?
4. What darkened Mark Twain in his old years?
5. Besides writing, what other jobs did Mark Twain take?

II. Translate into Chinese the following sentences taken from the passage.

1. He won a worldwide audience for his stories of the youthful adventures of Tom Sawyer and Huckleberry Finn.
2. The Civil War put an end to the steamboat traffic and Clemens moved to Virginia City to volunteer in the war on the side of Union, where he edited the *Territorial Enterprise*.
3. Even when there's obvious bitterness related to some of his experiences, he put

in the narrative with humor; even in tragedy, he's able to triumph through the power of language.

4. He has been called a realist and a romantic, a humorist and a satirist.

5. His mark on American literary history cannot be overstated.

III. Fill in the blanks with the words or phrases listed in Words and Expressions to Learn. Change the form where necessary.

1. Mark Twain won a _____ audience for his stories of the youthful adventures of Tom Sawyer and Huckleberry Finn.

2. He once _____ a licensed Mississippi river-boat pilot.

3. Mark Twain _____ in the war on the side of Union.

4. Mark Twain married Olivia Langdon in 1870, which provided him with enough _____ security.

5. There is obvious bitterness _____ some of Mark Twain's experiences.

6. The death of his wife and his second daughter _____ Mark Twain's life.

7. The book, *Huckleberry Finn* was once _____ by the government.

8. Through Mark Twain's books, we now share tragedies, _____, and adventures of his life.

IV. Complete the following sentences.

1. During that period liquor _____ (禁止销售) in most states of USA.

2. It is almost impossible _____ (再走一公里).

3. Because of several setbacks, he had to _____ (终止他在中国的事业).

4. He described in detail _____ (办公室所发生的事情).

5. New policy didn't spare the company from _____ (财务压力).

6. This film _____ (激发了) our enthusiasm of traveling in Tibet.

7. The black people _____ (过着悲惨的生活) at that time.

8. A lot of his predictions _____ (变成了现实).

Part IV Practical English

I.O.U and Receipt Forms（条据）I

借据和收条是我们借用或接受款项或物品时所打的条据,一般包括时间、正文、署名等几个部分。要求格式规范正确,表述简明扼要,用词准确达意。英语条据的立据时间须写在正文的右上角,立据人签名在右下角。

1. I.O.U（借据）

借据是人们把借物这一行为转化为书面文字表达出来的一种文体,属于一种简单的书信格式。借据上需写明钱物名称和数量、立据人及日期,其中所涉及的数据要准确,且不得涂改。

如:

> Sept. 16th, 2005
>
> Borrowed from the Foreign Language Department Reference Library a copy of *College English*.
>
> Wu Zhong

> 今借到外语系资料室《大学英语》一本。
>
> 吴中
> 2005年9月16日

2. Receipts（收据）

　　收据又称收条，是收到他人钱物后，给交钱或送物人立的字据，说明已经收到某物，可留作证据。收据上需写明钱物名称和数量、立据人及日期，不得涂改。收据的写法与借据大致相同。开头常以"Received from..."或"Received of..."引导，意思相当于汉语的"今收到……"或"收到……"。

如：

> Jan. 23rd, 2003
>
> Received from Student, Wang Zhihao one hundred *yuan* only for this month's tuition fee.
>
> Li Man
> For the Finance Office of Foreign Language Institute

> 今收到王志豪同学本月学费壹佰圆整。
>
> 李蔓
> 外语学院财务室
> 2003年1月23日

Useful Expressions

Borrowed from...	今借到……
I owe you (I.O.U)...	借到……
Received from...	今收到……
Received of...	收到……

Exercises

I. Fill in the blanks in the following I.O.U. in English so that it is functionally equivalent to the Chinese version.

今借到太平洋演艺中心二十根领带和六十件衬衫,此据。

张力
2005 年 12 月 24 日

December 24th, 2005
_____ the Pacific Showing Center _____ and sixty shirts.

Zhang Li

II. Translate the following Receipt into English with the guide of the samples.

今收到北大出版社《大学英语教程》第一册 150 本,此据。

宋和平
2006 年 2 月 7 日

Part V English Salon

Riddles

1. The land is white,
   The sea is black,
   It'll take a good scholar
   To riddle me that.
2. A slender man in white
   Walks on black soil all life.
   To teach the boys to write,
   It dies out in the strife.
3. It stands behind the door,
   With all the dirt in sight.
   When it walks on the floor,
   The room is clean and bright.

Requirement

Try to find the answer to each riddle.

Unit Five

Part I Text

 Guide to Text-Learning

1. Theme of the Text

We are happy to see computer go into many ordinary families and the Internet widely used at home. Obviously its uses are virtually beyond imagination. The World Wide Web, although still young, is deeply ingrained in our culture and everyday life. Have you ever thought of the reason why the network goes popular and how far it will go? Go ahead, read the text and think a little.

2. Words and Expressions Related to the Topic

Internet	因特网
World Wide Web	万维网
UNIX	一种多任务多用户操作系统
home application	家用
information	信息
be personalized	个性化、私密化
download	下载
on-line	在线
chat room	聊天室
become secure	变得安全

3. Grammatical Structures to Learn

(1) Sometimes it is even possible to **have** the selected articles **downloaded** to your hard disk while you sleep.

有时你还能趁睡觉的时间就把选好的文章下载到硬盘里。

(2) Home shopping is already popular and **enables** users **to** inspect the on-line catalogs of thousands of companies.

家庭网上购物早就开始流行，使人们能在网上查看多个公司的不同产品。

(3) **No doubt** the range of uses of computer networks will grow rapidly in the future, and probably in ways no one can now predict.

毋庸置疑，将来网络的应用领域还会迅速扩大，其增长方式现在也许还无法想象。

4. Grammar

Basic Sentence Patterns II: 1. SVO (主语+及物动词+宾语); 2. SVOO (主语+及物动词+间接宾语+直接宾语); 3. SVOO (主语+及物动词+直接宾语+直接宾语); 4. SVOC(主语+及物动词+宾语+宾语补足语)

5. Practical English

Bills (2): 1. Bills; 2. Invoices

Warming-Up Questions:

1. Have you ever used the Internet? If yes, what do you usually use it for? And how much time do you generally spend on the Internet each day?
2. Do you like to play any game in network? If so, could you give some examples?
3. Have you ever tried OICQ or QQ in chatting online? What's your nickname on the Internet, then?
4. What do you learn on the Internet?

Home Applications of Computer Networks

1   Why do people buy computers for home use? At the beginning, people own computers simply for word processing and games playing, but in recent years great changes have taken place completely. Probably the biggest reason is for Internet

access. Some of the more popular uses of the Internet for home users are as follows:

Access to remote information

2   Access to remote information comes in many forms. A person at home can visit the World Wide **Web** for information or just for fun. Information available includes the arts, business, cooking, government, health, history, hobbies, recreation, science, sports, travel, and many others. Fun comes in too many ways to mention.

3   Many newspapers have gone on-line and can be personalized. For example, it is sometimes possible to tell a newspaper that you want everything from political big events to common people's living conditions. Sometimes it is even possible to have the selected articles downloaded to your hard **disk** while you sleep or printed on your printer just before breakfast.

4   In addition to these is the on-line **digital** library. Many professional organizations already have many **journals** and **conference** proceedings on-line. Other groups are following rapidly. Depending on the cost, size, and weight of book-sized notebook computers, printed books may become out of date.

Person-to-person communication

5   All of the above applications involve interactions between a person and a remote database full of information. The second kind of network use is person-to-person communication. E-mail is already used on a daily basis by millions of people all over the world and its use is growing rapidly. It usually contains audio and video as well as text and pictures.

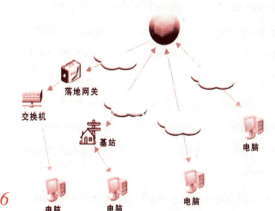

6   Many teenagers are keen on instant

---

access /'ækses/ *n.*
means or right of using, reaching, or obtaining entering
取得[接近]的方法[权利]等

remote /rɪ'məʊt/ *adj.*
distant in space or time
偏僻的,遥远的,远程的

web /web/ *n.*
a net of thin threads
网

disk /dɪsk/ *n.*
磁盘

digital /'dɪdʒɪtl/ *adj.*
数字的

journal /'dʒɜːnl/ *n.*
报纸,定期刊物(尤其涉及某一学科)

conference /'kɒnfərəns/ *n.*
a meeting for consultatio
会议,讨论会,协商会

messaging. This **facility**, **derived** from the UNIX talk program in use since around 1970, allows two people to type messages at each other in real time. A multi-person version of this idea is the chat room, in which a group of people can type messages for all to read.

Interactive entertainment

7   The third **range** about home application of computer networks is entertainment, which is a huge and growing industry. The killer application here is video on demand. A decade or so hence, it may be possible to select any movie or television program ever made, in any country, and have it displayed on your screen instantly. New films may become interactive, where the user is occasionally **prompted** for the story direction with alternative **versions** provided for all cases. Live television may also become interactive, with the audience participating in quiz shows.

Electronic commerce

8   Electronic commerce is now becoming the broadest sense of computer networks. Home shopping is already popular and enables users to inspect the on-line list of thousands of companies. Some will soon provide the ability to get an instant video on any product by just clicking on the product's name. After the customer buys a product **electronically** but cannot figure out how to use it, on-line technical support may be **consulted**.

9   Another area in which e-commerce is already happening is access to **financial** institutions. Many people already pay their bills, manage their bank accounts, and handle their investments electronically, which will surely grow as networks become more secure.

10   No doubt the range of uses of computer networks will grow rapidly in the future, and probably in ways no one can now **predict**. Computer networks may

---

facility /fə'sɪlɪti/ *n.*
设施,设备

derive /dɪ'raɪv/ *v.*
come from; have as an origin
得自,起源

range /reɪndʒ/ *n.*
the limits within which something operates or exists
范围,领域

prompt /prɒmpt/ *v.*
help by suggesting how to continue
提醒,提醒,指示

version /'vɜːʃən/ *n.*
a form of a written or musical work
版本

electronic /ɪlek'trɒnɪk/ *adj.*
of, or concerned with electrons
电子的

consult /kən'sʌlt/ *v.*
go to(a book, etc.) for information
查阅[书籍等],向[专业人士]咨询,请教

financial /faɪ'nænʃəl/ *adj.*
of, or relating to finance or finances
财政的,金融的

predict /prɪ'dɪkt/ *v.*
make a prediction about; tell in advance
预知,预言,预报

become hugely important to people who are geographically challenged, giving them the same access to services as people living in the middle of a big city.

(585 words)

Useful Phrases

in addition to	besides; as well as	除……之外,还
depend on	vary according to; be decided by	依赖,依靠,取决于 随……而定
full of	filled completely	满的
on a daily basis	everyday	每天(指一起共事的)
as well as	in addition to	此外,也,和
be keen on	love / mad about	喜欢,热爱,醉心于
derive from	come from	取得,起源,由来
on demand		在线(在要求时,一经请求时)
figure out	work out	算出,想出;理解;断定;解决

Reading Aloud and Memorizing the Following

I. Read the following paragraph taken from the text until you learn it by heart.

No doubt the range of uses of computer networks will grow rapidly in the future, and probably in ways no one can now predict. Computer networks may become hugely important to people who are geographically challenged, giving them the same access to services as people living in the middle of a big city.

Comprehension of the Text

II. Complete each of the following sentences with the most appropriate word or words from the four choices marked A, B, C and D.

1. Why do people buy computers for home use in recent years?
   A. For word processing.
   B. For games playing.
   C. For decorating their house.
   D. For accessory remote information.

2. With the development of the on-line digital library, printed books will be out of date because _____.
   A. it's very popular
   B. it's a little bit common
   C. it's unnoticed
   D. it's not very important

3. The type of person-to-person communication which is favored by teenagers is _____.
   A. instant messaging
   B. peer-to-peer communication
   C. E-Mail
   D. A and B

4. _____ did the UNIX talk program is used.
   A. Long before 1970
   B. Around 1970
   C. After 1980
   D. Nearly 1990

5. According to the text, which one is not included in electronic commerce?
   A. Shopping on-line.
   B. Financial institutions.
   C. Electronic flea markets.
   D. Supermarket.

III. Answer the following questions with the information you've got from the text.

1. Traditionally, what do people usually do on the computer?   (Para. 1)
2. After reading about this passage, what kind of reading do you want to choose?   (Para. 2—4)
3. To teenagers, what is their favorite activity on line?   (Para. 6)
4. Does the Internet bring great changes to people's entertainment life? And how?   (Para. 7)
5. From the text, how many ranges about home application of computer networks are mentioned? And what are they?   (The whole text)

Vocabulary

IV. Find the definition in column B which matches the words or expressions in column A.

A	B
1. remote	(　) a. everyday
2. conference	(　) b. different form or copy
3. range	(　) c. eager or enthusiastic
4. figure out	(　) d. besides
5. consult	(　) e. confer with
6. predict	(　) f. foretell
7. on a daily basis	(　) g. work out
8. in addition to	(　) h. a gun-firing distance
9. version	(　) i. meeting
10. keen on	(　) j. distant

V. Fill in the blanks with the words given in the brackets. Change the form where necessary.

1. It isn't _____ possible that you will be chosen to go. (remote)
2. The earthquake _____ several months before. (predict)
3. In business, when you are caught by big problems, you should always _____ your partners. (consult)
4. We could take the train or _____ go by car. (alternative)
5. The customs officer _____ my passport. (inspect)
6. We are still _____ moving house. (process)
7. He is a popular television _____. (entertain)
8. Thousands of English words _____ Latin. (derive)
9. _____ the name of the list there are six other applicants. (addition)
10. He _____ to be told everything. (demand)

VI. Complete each of the following sentences with the most appropriate word or words from the four choices marked A, B, C and D.

1. _____ another chance, I will certainly pass the driving test.
   A. Give   B. Giving   C. To give   D. Given

2. We think _____ impossible for them to finish their assignment in such a short time.
   A. it   B. what   C. this   D. that

3. A good writer is _____ who can express the commonplace in an uncommon way.
   A. that   B. it   C. this   D. one

4. _____ nobody was very enthusiastic about the trip, they decided to cancel it.
   A. For   B. Why   C. Seeing that   D. Concerning that

5. A man escaped from the prison last week. It was a long time _____ the guards discovered what had happened.
   A. since   B. before   C. when   D. until

6. Criticism and self-criticism is necessary _____ it helps us to correct our mistakes.
   A. until   B. unless   C. in that   D. in which

7. There was so much noise that the speaker couldn't make himself _____.
   A. heard   B. to hear   C. hearing   D. being heard

8. The new power station is reported _____ within three years.
   A. to complete   C. to have completed
   B. having been completed   D. to have been completed

9. Jack was so _____ the computer game that he didn't notice my arrival.
   A. grateful to   B. absorbed in   C. thoughtful of   D. associated with

10. Eating too much fat can _____ heart disease and cause high blood pressure.
    A. contribute to B. refer to   C. attend to   D. devote to

Structure

VII. Rewrite the following sentences after the models.

Model 1   You may download the selected article to your hard disk while you are sleep.

You may **have** the selected articles **downloaded** to your hard disk while you sleep.

1. She asked her cousin to repair her web camera.
2. In order to hunt for a job, some graduates print out their resume.
3. The builders have to complete the Bird's Nest for Beijing 2008 Olympic Games in advance.
4. When he was away on business, he often washed his clothes in the laundry.
5. We cannot run our computer when it is attacked by virus.

Model 2   People may use mobile phones to surf the Internet.

Mobile phones **enable** people to surf the Internet.

1. I gave him full directions to help him to find the house.
2. The bus company resumed normal bus services after reaching a reasonable agreement.
3. Viruses protection is a practical way to protect our computer.
4. The new subway makes it easier to get to the stadium.
5. With the help of software, we may get access to the Internet in seconds.

VIII. Study the model and translate the following sentences into English.

Model   **No doubt** the range of uses of computer networks will grow rapidly in the future, and probably in ways no one can now predict.

1. 毫无疑问,互联网是全世界最便利的工具了。
2. 这部片子肯定会破票房记录,这点毋庸置疑。
3. 音乐无疑是最为通用的世界语言。
4. 他到达那里时必定会给我们打电话。
5. 这无疑是我们迄今为止最有用的一次会议。

Translation

IX. Translate the following sentences into Chinese.

1. Electronic commerce is now becoming the broadest sense of computer networks.

2. Sometimes it is even possible to have the selected articles downloaded to your hard disk while you sleep or printed on your printer just before breakfast.

3. The third range about home application of computer networks is entertainment, which is a huge and growing industry.

4. Home shopping is already popular and enables users to inspect the on-line list of thousands of companies.

5. No doubt the range of uses of computer networks will grow rapidly in the future.

X. Translate the following sentences into English using the words or phrases in the brackets.

1. 在这个价格范围内,有好几种汽车可供选购。(range)

2. 我去向他请教,他爱理不理的,不太愿意帮助我。(consult)

3. 经济学家预言通货膨胀率将会增长。(predict)

4. 这次事故除了伤亡之外,还有多人失踪。(in addition to)

5. 报纸上尽是些关于王室成员的趣闻逸事的报道。(full of)

Part II Grammar

Basic Sentence Patterns（基本句型）II

4. **Subject+Vt.+Object (Noun/Pronoun)**

  We study   English.
  I   know   him very well.
  They play   football after class.

5. **Subject+Vt.+Indirect Object (Noun/Pronoun)+Direct Object (Noun)**

  He gave the little boy a toy gun.
  I   bought her   a new bike.
  Mary has told the boy   the truth.

注：① 有些及物动词，如 give, tell 等，可以有两个宾语。一般说来，这两个宾语一个指物，一个指人；指物的叫直接宾语，指人的叫间接宾语，间接宾语一般放在直接宾语之前。

② 当间接宾语后置时，通常在它前面要添加相应的介词。如：

  I gave some money to the old man.

  He bought a new dictionary for me.

③ 通常可以带双宾语的动词有：ask, bring, buy, call, do, get, give, lend, offer, send, teach, tell, etc.

6. **Subject + Vt. + Direct Object (Noun / Pronoun) + Direct Object (Noun)**

  He taught me   English.

这类可以带双直接宾语的动词有 answer, ask, envy, save, teach, etc.

7. **Subject+Vt.+Object (Noun/Pronoun)+Complement (Noun/Adjective/Infinitive)**

  I   found Tommy   a good student.
  They call   him   Little Tom.
  I   wanted her   to come.
  We saw   him   go out.

注：① 英语中有些及物动词的直接宾语后面需要加个补足语，句子的意思才

算完整。宾语和它的补足语在逻辑上有主谓关系,合在一起叫复合宾语。

② 可带复合宾语的动词有 ask, tell, see, make, want, call 等。常用作宾语补足语的有名词、形容词、动词不定式等。

1. Complete each of the following sentences with the most appropriate word or words from the four choices marked A, B, C and D.

1. There _____ no water or air on the moon.
   A. is   B. are   C. has   D. have
2. Everyone in the class _____ very happy.
   A. is   B. are   C. am   D. were
3. A woman with her husband, both looking anxious, _____ the guard to let them through.
   A. asks   B. was asked   C. was asking   D. were asking
4. Mr. Haines will give his workers _____.
   A. new instructions   B. for new instructions
   C. of new instructions   D. to new instructions
5. Prof. Li taught _____.
   A. us with English   B. us English
   C. English with us   D. English us
6. _____ are a hardworking people.
   A. The Germany B. The German   C. The Germans D. The Germen
7. I have never met _____ man.
   A. a so careless B. so a careless C. a such careless D. such a careless
8. The singer and dancer _____ our evening.
   A. is to attend   B. are to attend   C. were to attend   D. is attended
9. Half of the fruit _____ bad. I don't want any of it.
   A. has gone   B. was   C. have gone   D. is gone

10. The beautiful _____ us _____.
    A. gives, pleasure   B. give, pleasure
    C. gave, pleased   D. will give, pleasant

II. Translate the following into English.

1. 她把雨伞忘在教室里了。

2. 你必须给她弄点吃的。

3. 你已经帮了我大忙。

4. 大家都管他叫胆小鬼。

5. 董事们选举约翰为银行经理。

III. Fill in the blanks with the words given in the box in their proper forms.

| he | admire | old | stay | simple |
| success | fail | ever | send | to |

1. Although he had made his great effort, the project proved a _____.
2. He _____ by every one around him.
3. The walk in space was great _____.
4. We all called _____ Lao Li.
5. Her parents _____ her to study abroad.
6. The heavy rain made us _____ at home the whole day.
7. I am glad to show the way to our college _____ them.
8. We _____ want him to pay the basic fee.

Part III Reading Practice

Guide to Reading

1. Words and Expressions to Learn

cyber	n.	电脑技术
date	v.	约会
cyberspace	n.	网络空间
romance	n.	传奇文学；风流韵事
polish	v.	擦亮，磨光；推敲
significant	adj.	有意义的，重要的
intellectual	adj.	智力的，有智力的
deprive	v.	剥夺，使丧失
emotional	adj.	情绪的，情感的
superior	adj.	较高的，上级的
bind	v.	定；系；缔结
all of a sudden		突然
have sth in common		在……有共同之处

2. Pre-Reading Questions

(1) Have you ever met anyone showing love to you on the Internet?
(2) Do you believe cyber-love or not?

What is Cyber Love?

1   Cyber dating, cyber love... most people may feel so fresh with these terms. A guy "meets" a girl in a chatting room; they find out that they have so much in

common. And from all the chatting and meeting online, all of a sudden they discover that they cannot **sleep tight**(睡得很香) anymore without saying good night to their cyber lovers.

2   How does a cyber love vary from a real life romance? Cyber love is not the love of parents or friends but the affection, attachment and care toward a person of opposite sex.  Perhaps one significant difference is that communication plays such a large part. Words that convey feelings have enormous effect. Before a real date we fix our hair and our clothes, while on the Internet we polish our intellect, imagination and personality. Actually the **sequence** (*n.* 顺序) is **reversed** (*v.* 颠倒)—first we show our inner beauty and only after it has won victory does the **veil** (*n.* 面纱) fall off the physical vehicle of that personality at the time of that first meeting in person.

3   It is a popular topic in cyberspace to debate whether or not true love can develop merely on an intellectual level, which is without the physical attraction, the familiarity of the other's appearance. To put it another way: does the physical appearance of the man or woman play a part in the relationship if they have already fell in love through the **exchange** (*n.* 交流) of thoughts and feelings?

4   Many people say it is against the nature of love because cyber love deprives people of the sense of sight, **facial** (*adj.* 面部的) expression and body language. On the other hand, there are those who favor Internet relationships claiming that the emotional relationship that develops in such a way is superior to mere physical attraction.

5   Whatever opinions may be on cyber love, it must be said that the power of Internet has proved strong enough to bring together lovers who have few opportunities to meet in the real world because of distance or even financial **barriers** (*n.* 障碍).

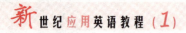

6   Love comes easily on the Internet, and goes away easily too. But that doesn't mean cyber dating and cyber love do not exist.

7   If love is a seed, the Internet is just the wind, your heart is the water and life itself is the soil.

Reading Comprehension

I. Answer the following questions according to the passage.

1. Why does communication play a significant role in cyber-love?
2. What does the word "veil" mean in the last sentence of the first paragraph?
3. Is physical appearance important in cyber-love?
4. What binds the writer of this passage and the German chimney sweep?
5. What's your opinion about cyber-love?

II. Translate into Chinese the following sentences taken from the passage.

1. Words that convey feelings have enormous effect.
2. First we show our inner beauty and only after it has won victory does the veil fall off the physical vehicle of that personality at the time of that first meeting in person.
3. Does the physical appearance of the man or woman play a part in the relationship if they have already fell in love through the exchange of thoughts and feelings?
4. Many people say it is against the nature of love because cyber love deprives people of the sense of sight, facial expression and body language.
5. It must be said that the power of the Internet has proved strong enough to bring together lovers who have few opportunities to meet in the real world because of distance or even financial barriers.

III. Fill in the blanks with the words or phrases listed in Words and Expressions to Learn. Change the form where necessary.

1. His essay needs _____.
2. She _____ of schooling at ten.
3. _____ someone shouted, "It's two minutes past twelve!"
4. Her parents were highly qualified _____.
5. He _____ (as an) apprentice to a shoe-maker.
6. This western restaurant _____ the one we went to last week.
7. He had nothing _____ with us.
8. She was very _____. She cried even when her husband left for another city on business.

IV. Complete the following sentences.

1. It is polite to _____ our hairs and clothes before we date with others (修理、整理).
2. We may get many useful information _____ (从网上).
3. I think cyber love _____ (与……不同) from a real life romance.
4. The man _____ (举足轻重) in the team.
5. Soon she _____ (爱上了) with a village doctor.
6. He is _____ (够壮实) to bear this hard work.
7. It is well known that true love comes from _____ (信任和宽容).
8. One's _____ (外表) does tell us something.

Part IV   Practical English

Bills（单据）II

3. Bills（账单）

在商店或其他地方购物后,顾客便会得到商家出示的购物清单,即账单。账单是一种非常简单的文体。

写账单时,注意要把各个栏目排列清楚,并写明所购买的商品的价格,也要注意时间、地点、姓名等。

如:

Bill

Mr. George Bush,

Bought from QinTai Gallery:

1. Chinese Painting   U.S.$ 1500
2. Frame for the above   U.S.$ 200

             Total: U.S.$ 1700

账 单

乔治·布什 先生

在琴台画廊购得

1. 中国画一幅   价值:1500 美元
2. 画框一个   价值:200 美元
                         总计:1700 美元

4. Invoices（发票）

发票是收付款项或货物的凭据，也是出具货物名称、数量、价格等内容的清单。因此填写发票时要求字迹清楚，不得涂改。

发票是印好了的表格，使用时只需填写人名、单位名称、地址、数额、日期等。

如：

Chengdu Book Store

Retail Invoice
Feb. 7th, 2006

Code: 151010521004
No. 04253896

Name of Buyer: Li Yixuan

Goods Name	Copies Bought	Unit Price	Amount (RMB)
The Story of My Life	1	22.00	22.00
Charlotte's Web	1	17.00	17.00
Total			39.00

Seller: Luo Xi

成都布克书店

发票代码 151010521004
发票号码 04253896

客户名称：李艺轩　　　2006年2月7日

品名	数量	单价	金额
《我的生活》	1（本）	22.00 元	22.00 元
《夏洛的网》	1（本）	17.00 元	17.00 元
金额合计（大写）			叁拾玖圆整

收款员： 罗希

Exercises

I. *Fill in the blanks in the following English bill so that it is functionally equivalent to the Chinese version.*

账　单

汤姆·杰克逊先生

在百盛购物中心购得

1. 西装一套　　　　　　价值：1750 元
2. 太阳镜一副　　　　　价值：320 元
3. 皮鞋一双　　　　　　价值：540 元
　　　　　　　　　　　总计：2610 元

Bill

Mr. Tom Jackson,

　　_____ Parkson Shopping Center:

1. _____　　　　　　1750 *yuan*
2. _____　　　　　　320 *yuan*
3. _____　　　　　　540 *yuan*
　　　　　　　　　Total: 2610 *yuan*

II. *Write an invoice to show Mr. Tom Jackson that he has bought the goods from Parkson Shopping Center according to the information above in English.*

Part V English Salon

Funny Questions

1. What kind of clothing lasts the longest?
2. What is the coldest place in a cinema?
3. What has a neck but no throat?
4. What table do we often see in fields?
5. What country is good at skating?
6. I'm something that can run but can't walk. What am I?
7. What is it that you can't see, but is always before you?
8. What is it that has legs but can't walk?

Answer the questions in your own way and give the reason.

Unit Six

Part I Text

Guide to Text-Learning

1. Theme of the Text

The Olympic Games are an international event of summer and winter sports, in which thousands of athletes compete in a wide variety of events. The Games are currently held every two years, with Summer and Winter Olympic Games alternating. The 2008 Summer Olympics, officially known as the Games of the XXIX Olympiad, were a major international multi-sport event that took place in Beijing, China, from August 8 to August 24, 2008.

2. Words and Expressions Related to the Topic

the opening ceremony	开幕式
host nation	东道国
torch relay	火炬接力
the Olympic Flag	奥运会会旗
take the oath	宣誓
medal ceremonies	颁奖仪式
IOC	国际奥委会
Olympic ideals	奥林匹克精神
the national anthem	国歌

3. Grammatical Structures to Learn

(1) The Olympic Games have always included a number of ceremonies, **many of which** emphasize the themes of international friendship and peaceful cooperation.

历届奥林匹克运动会都有一些仪式，其中许多仪式都强调国际友谊以及和平合作的主题。

(2) **It is supposed to** take place as soon as possible after each event.
颁奖仪式应该在比赛项目结束时立即进行。

(3) It is eagerly expected and well **attended**.
人们急切企盼,踊跃参加(奥运会开幕式)。

4. Grammar

基本句型转换 I:疑问句 (Interrogative Sentences)

5. Practical English

Notices

Warming-Up Questions:

1. Do you have any ideas about Olympic Games?
2. Can you give a detailed description of the Olympic Flag?
3. List some Chinese gold medal winners of the Olympic Games.

Ceremonies of the Olympic Games

1   The Olympic Games have always included a number of ceremonies, many of which **emphasize** the **themes** of international friendship and peaceful **cooperation**.

2   The **traditional** part of the ceremonies starts with a parade of nations, during which the **athletes** march into the stadium country by country. Usually a top athlete from each country carries the flag of his or her nation.

emphasize /ˈemfəsaiz/ *v.*
say sth in a strong way
强调
theme /θiːm/ *n.*
main subject or idea
主题,题目
cooperation /kəuˌɔpəˈreiʃən/ *n.*
acting or working together for a common purpose
合作,协作
traditional /trəˈdiʃn(ə)l/ *adj.*
of, relating to, or in accord with tradition
传统的,惯例的
athlete /ˈæθliːt/ *n.*
those competing in sports competitions
运动员,运动选手

Because of its historical **status** as the origin of the Olympics, the Greek team always enters first, and the team of the host nation enters last. Over the years the opening ceremony has developed into a complex and expensive entertainment, with music, speeches, and dances. It is eagerly expected and well attended. The torch relay, in which the Olympic Flame **symbolizes** the passing of Olympic traditions, was **introduced** as part of the opening ceremony at the 1936 Summer Games in Berlin. In the relay the torch is lit in Olympia, Greece, and is carried over several weeks or months from there to the host city by a series of runners. After the last runner has lit the Olympic Flame in the main Olympic stadium, the host country's head of state declares the Games officially open, and doves are **released** as a symbol of peace.

3 The Olympic Flag, with its five rings of different colors against a white background, was flown for the first time at the 1920 Games in Antwerp, Belgium. The rings of the upper row are, from left to right, blue, black and red. The rings of the lower row are yellow and green. The five rings represent unity among the nations of Africa, the Americas, Asia, Australia, and Europe.

4 Also in 1920 the first **reciting** of the Olympic Oath was taken. One athlete from the host country takes the oath at the opening ceremony on behalf of all the athletes. The chosen athlete holds a corner of the Olympic Flag while repeating the oath: "In the name of all competitors, I promise that we shall take part in these Olympic Games, respecting and abiding by

---

status /ˈsteitəs/ n.
position relative to that of others
地位,身份

symbolize /ˈsimbəlaiz/ v.
serve as a symbol of
象征

introduce /ˌintrəˈdjuːs/ v.
bring in and establish in a new place or environment
引进,传入

release /riˈliːs/ v.
let go
释放

recite /riˈsait/ v.
say aloud from memory, esp. to an audience
背诵;朗诵

the rules that govern them, in the true spirit of sportsmanship, for the glory of sport and the honor of our teams."

5   Medal ceremonies are also an important part of the Games. It is supposed to take place as soon as possible after each **event**. The winner stands on the central step of the platform, with the second-place winner on the right and the third-place winner on the left. Their names are announced and the medals are presented by either the IOC president or another IOC member. The flags of the medalists' countries are raised, with the winner's flag on the central of the three flagpoles, and the national anthem of the gold medalist's nation is played.

> **event** /i'vent/ *n.*
> a contest or an item in a sports programme
> 比赛项目
> **parade** /pə'reid/ *n.*
> a public procession to celebrate sth
> 游行，列队行进
> **stadium** /'steidiəm/ *n.*
> a large, usually open structure for sports events
> 体育场，运动场
> **global** /'gləubəl/ *adj.*
> including the whole world
> 全球的，全世界的

6   Originally there was another **parade** of nations during the closing ceremonies of the Games. At the end of the 1956 Summer Games in Melbourne, Australia, however, the athletes, not separated into national teams, entered the **stadium** together during the closing ceremony, as a symbol of **global** unity. And this custom was continued. After the athletes join in the main Olympic stadium, the president of the IOC invites the athletes and spectators to meet again at the site of the next Games and declares the Games end, and the Olympic Flame is put out.

(550 words)

Useful Phrases

a number of	many	许多
develop into	change gradually over a long period of time	演变，变成
a series of	(informal) a lot of	大量，许多
on behalf of	instead of someone, or as their representative	代表
in the name of	because you believe in sth	以……的名义，凭

abide by	accept and obey a decision, rule, agreement etc.	遵守；坚持
put out	stop... from burning	使……熄灭，扑灭

Notes

1 Greek

希腊是奥运会的发祥地，有史记载的第一届奥运会于公元前 776 年在希腊举行。

2 Olympia

奥林匹亚位于希腊首都雅典西南 300 公里的丘陵地区，现代奥运会的圣火都在此点燃，她是奥林匹克运动的象征之一。

3 "In the name of all competitors, I promise that we shall take part in these Olympic Games, respecting and abiding by the rules that govern them, in the true spirit of sportsmanship, for the glory of sport and the honor of our teams." "代表所有参赛运动员，我宣誓我们参加本次奥运会，尊重并遵守大会各项规则，恪守体育道德，为体育争光，为团体争光。"

Exercises

Reading Aloud and Memorizing the Following

I. Read the following paragraph taken from the text until you learn it by heart.

    The Olympic Flag, with its five rings of different colors against a white background, was flown for the first time. The rings of the upper row are, from left to right, blue, black and red. The rings of the lower row are yellow and green. The five rings represent unity among the nations of Africa, the Americas, Asia, Australia, and Europe.

Comprehension of the Text

II. Choose the best answer to each of the following questions according to the passage.

1. According to the passage, the last nation entering the Olympic stadium in 2008 would be _____.
   A. the United States B. China C. Greece D. Zambia
2. Lighting the Olympic Flame became a part of Olympic ceremony in _____.
   A. the 1956 Summer Games in Melbourne
   B. the 1920 Games in Antwerp, Belgium
   C. the 1936 Summer Games in Berlin
   D. the 1972 Munich Olympics
3. The ceremony innovations in 1920 include _____.
   A. raising the Olympic Flag   B. lighting the Olympic Flame
   C. reciting the Olympic Oath   D. both A and C
4. Medals are awarded to _____.
   A. the first-place winner   B. the second-place winner
   C. the third-place winner   D. all of the above
5. The following statements are true except for _____.
   A. the start-point of the torch relay is in Greece.
   B. medal ceremony is held immediately after each event
   C. only the national anthem of the gold medalist's nation is played at the medal ceremony
   D. the head of state of the host country declares the Olympic Games end

III. Answer the following questions with the information you've got from the text.

1. What are the themes of the Olympic ceremonies? (Para. 1)
2. What does the Olympic Flame symbolize? (Para. 2)

3. When and where did the Olympic Flag first appear at the opening ceremony? (Para. 3)

4. What does the Olympic Oath mainly demonstrate? (Para. 4)

5. In which way the parade at the closing ceremony is different from that at the opening ceremony? (Para. 6)

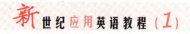

IV. Find the definition in column B which matches the words or expressions in column A.

A	B
1. subject	( ) a. sportsman
2. be supposed to	( ) b. be involved in
3. status	( ) c. serious promise
4. recite	( ) d. social, legal or professional position
5. origin	( ) e. should
6. innovation	( ) f. say from memory
7. oath	( ) g. source
8. develop into	( ) h. develop and change gradually
9. take part in	( ) i. making changes
10. athlete	( ) j. topic

V. Fill in the blanks with the words given in the brackets. Change the form where necessary.

1. The _____ price of the car was a bit too high. (origin)

2. She played the piano for our _____. (entertain)

3. Women are questioning their _____ role in society, as wives and mothers. (tradition)

4. The Olympic gold _____ was welcomed as a hero at the airport. (medal)

5. The railroad station is in the _____ part of the city. (center)

6. Was King Arthur a real _____ figure? (history)

7. Brothers and sisters should live together in _____. (unite)

8. The two boys formed a deep and lasting _____. (friend)
9. Their ability to _____ has allowed them to compete in world markets. (innovation)
10. We try to teach the kids to have good _____. (sportsman)

VI. *Complete each of the following sentences with the most appropriate word or words from the four choices marked A, B, C and D.*

1. She works _____ a secretary in that company.
   A. on   B. in   C. as   D. at
2. Will you be home _____ the summer vacation?
   A. over   B. across   C. on   D. with
3. The younger policeman was leaning _____ the desk.
   A. on   B. to   C. for   D. against
4. They arrived _____ we were having dinner.
   A. before   B. after   C. while   D. soon after
5. The teacher explained the text sentence _____ sentence.
   A. for   B. after   C. from   D. by
6. The group gradually developed _____ a political party.
   A. to   B. into   C. up   D. for
7. He was educated at the local school, after _____ he went on to Peking University.
   A. that   B. which   C. it   D. whom
8. Women's social _____ hasn't changed much over the years.
   A. location   B. state   C. statement   D. status
9. She's the kind of person you either love _____ hate.
   A. and   B. also   C. or   D. nor
10. AIDS became widespread in the 1980s, but no one is certain of its _____.
    A. date   B. time   C. origin   D. result

Structure

VII. Rewrite the following sentences after the models.

Model 1   We should check out of the hotel by 11 o'clock.

We **are supposed** to check out of the hotel by 11 o'clock.

1. I should not tell anyone.
2. When are you expected to be there?
3. You shouldn't take the books out of the room.
4. Nobody should smoke in the building.
5. We should abide by the school rules.

Model 2   It is an old room, and I was born in the room twenty years ago.

It is an old room **in which** I was born twenty years ago.

1. I'm looking forward to the summer vacation. During the summer vacation I'll go sightseeing in Europe.
2. This is a fantastic book. I found much information about Greek history in the book.
3. She attended the meeting and she met several old friends at the meeting.
4. This is a difficult question. We've had so much discussion about it.
5. The workers are building the stadium. The Olympic ceremonies will be held in the stadium.

VIII. Study the model and translate the following sentences into English.

Model   He decided to **attend** the meeting in person.

1. 孩子已到了该上学的年龄。(attend school)
2. 我们今天下午要听一个微生物学的讲座。(attend a lecture)
3. 他们每个星期天都要做礼拜。(attend church)
4. 我们一家人下星期天要去参加约翰和伊丽莎白的婚礼。(attend a wedding)
5. 本次讲座听者众多。(well attended)

Translation

IX. Translate the following sentences into Chinese.

1. The traditional part of the ceremonies starts with a parade of nations, during which the athletes march into the stadium country by country.

2. One athlete from the host country takes the oath at the opening ceremony on behalf of all the athletes.

3. Their names are announced and the medals are presented by either the IOC president or another IOC member.

4. It is supposed to take place as soon as possible after each event.

5. The five rings represent unity among the nations of Africa, the Americas, Asia, Australia, and Europe.

X. Translate the following sentences into English using the words or phrases in the brackets.

1. 这家工厂成为了国际知名的大公司。(develop into)

2. 我们已经是多年的好朋友了。(a number of)

3. 他代表班上全体同学给报社编辑写了一封感谢信。(on behalf of)

4. 大约20名同学参加了演讲比赛。(take part in)

5. 我们一定会遵守诺言。(abide by)

Part II Grammar

基本句型转换 I

Interrogative Sentences（疑问句）

具有询问或怀疑语气的句子叫疑问句。就其句法结构和交际功能来说，疑问句主要有四种类型。它们是一般疑问句、特殊疑问句、选择疑问句和附加疑问句。

类型（Type）	概要（Definition）	例句（Examples）
一般疑问句 (General Question)	就某事提出疑问的句子叫一般疑问句。	1. Are you Mr. John from America? 2. Has she a dancing for dancing? 3. Did the manager attend the meeting? 4. Will you go on a trip this summer? 5. Can she recite the texts in the book?
特殊问句 (Special Question)	对陈述句中的某一成分用疑问词提问的句子叫特殊疑问句，一般读降调。疑问词包括疑问代词 what, which, whose 和疑问副词 when, where, why, how 等。	1. Who have English classes on Monday morning? 2. What has happened? 3. What classes do you have on Monday mornings? 4. Which do you prefer? 5. When do you have English classes?
选择问句 (Alternative Question)	提出两种或以上的情况供对方选择的疑问句，回答时要具体。	1. —Will you play football or read in the library after class? 　—I will play basketball. 2. —Do you like apples or pears? 　—Both, I think.
附加疑问句 (Tag Question)	说话人对自己提出的想法和情况较有把握，或问话的目的只是希望对方来赞同或证实所陈述的事情。它由陈述句加简略问句构成，中间有逗号隔开。在通常情况下，如果陈述句部分是肯定结构，疑问部分须用否定结构，反之亦然。	1. The watch is fast, isn't it? 2. The watch isn't fast, is it? 3. They can't go with me, can they? 4. Give me a hand, will/would you? 5. Let's sing the song together, shall we? 6. I suppose you're not going today, are you? 7. He could hardly speak, could he?

Exercises

I. Ask questions on the underlined parts of the following sentences.

1. I went to see my parents <u>last weekend</u>.

2. <u>The famous professor</u> gave us a lecture about Chinese history.

3. Jane went to bed early <u>because she was tired</u>.

4. <u>Twenty</u> people were killed in the accident.

5. Many students in the countryside go to school <u>on foot</u>.

II. Add a suitable question tag to each of the following statement.

1. You had a discussion about the football match, _____?
2. Buy me a Chinese-English dictionary when you go to the bookshop, _____?
3. She hasn't been to Europe, _____?
4. There are many tourists during the vacation, _____?
5. John seldom sings, _____?

III. Rewrite the following sentences as required.

1. Jack owns a shoe factory in the city. (Turn it into a general question.)

2. She wrote to me every week. (Turn it into a general question.)

3. They are going to the movie tonight. (Turn it into a general question.)

4. Catherine likes tea and coffee. (Turn it into an alternative question.)

5. Tom is good at playing the violin and the piano. (Turn it into an alternative question.)

_____

Part III Reading Practice

 Guide to Reading

1. Words and Expressions to Learn

mascot	n.	吉祥物,吉祥符
incredible	adj.	难以置信的,〈口〉惊人的;极妙的
deserve	v.	应受(到),该得(到)
appreciation	n.	感谢
blessing	n.	祝福
prosperity	n.	兴旺,繁荣,昌盛
passion	n.	热情,激情
touch	vt.	感动;触动
the Five Friendlies		2008年奥组委为奥运会吉祥物五福娃取的英文名
Jacques Rogge		雅克·罗格
Lausanne		洛桑(瑞士西部城市,国际奥委会总部所在地)

2. Pre-Reading Questions

(1) Do you know anything about the Official Mascots of the Beijing 2008 Olympic Games?

(2) List the names of the Five Friendlies.

Letter from IOC President Jacques Rogge

1 Hello Beijing, hello China.

2   Greetings from Lausanne.

3   And a special hello to all the children and young people who may be watching this show because this day is for you! By now you've met your new little friends—the Five Friendlies.

4   I've been making friends with new Olympic mascots for about 40 years. And so I can say that this is a great day on China's Olympic journey.

5   The Five Friendlies are an incredible little family, chosen carefully by Beijing 2008 to represent all of China, and to carry a message of friendship to the children of the world.

6   Beijing is lucky to have so many beautiful animals to represent the Olympic spirit. When I look at this little group, I see joy. I see kids playing. And I see fun, lots of fun. The great Chinese artists who created these characters deserve our appreciation and the thanks of children everywhere. I love them all. And I love the story that they're carrying traditional Chinese blessings all over the world.

7   If I've got my Chinese mythology right, Beibei will bring you prosperity. Jingjing will bring you happiness. Huanhuan will fill you with passion. Yingying will give you good health. And Nini will bring you good luck. How's a great blessing!

8   And I can't wait till they come to visit me in Lausanne. I can see in their smiles that they love fun and games. And I'm sure they'll get along really well with all my friends here. I believe that this little family of Friendlies—the fish, the panda, the flame, the **antelope** (*n.* 藏羚羊) and the **swallow** (*n.* 燕子)—will become the most popular mascots

in Olympic history, especially when the children of China begin to play with them.

9   And now as I end this message, let me offer my congratulations to the leadership of Beijing 2008 for selecting such a great and friendly group of mascots.

10   You've certainly touched my heart with your choices. And I'm sure the Five Friendlies will touch the heart of the world.

11   Thank you and have a great day in China.

Reading Comprehension

I. Answer the following questions according to the passage.

1. What's the Chinese sentence when you put the first part of the names of the Five Friendlies together?
2. What does the name of the Five Friendlies suggest?
3. What blessings does each mascot represent?
4. Four of the five mascots are animals, what are they?
5. What is the author's attitude toward the Five Friendlies?

II. Translate into Chinese the following sentences taken from the passage.

1. And so I can say that this is a tremendous day on China's Olympic journey.
2. The Five Friendlies are an incredible little family, chosen carefully by Beijing 2008 to represent all of China, and to carry a message of friendship to the children of the world.
3. The great Chinese artists who created these characters deserve our appreciation and the thanks of children everywhere.
4. And I'm sure they'll get along really well with all my friends here.
5. You've certainly touched my heart with your choices.

III. Fill in the blanks with the words or phrases listed in Words and Expressions to Learn. Change the form where necessary.

1. Her sufferings have _____ the hearts of people in the country.
2. We wish you health, happiness, and _____.
3. For such a tiny woman she had a(n) _____ appetite.
4. Please accept my _____ upon your marriage.
5. The organizing committee has also issued a document calling for designs for the _____ of the games.
6. They sang with great _____.
7. He _____ this glory.
8. They cost a _____ amount of money.

IV. Complete the following sentences.

1. He may _____ (在看 NBA) in the dormitory.
2. It's a great honor for me to _____ (表示祝贺) the graduates in 2009.
3. He is one of _____ (最讨人喜欢) students in the class.
4. He _____ (值得) a reward for his efforts.
5. He is a difficult man to _____ (相处).

Part IV   Practical English

Notices (通知)

通知是单位、团体以及个人向大众告知某一事情的简短文字,通常刊登在报刊或张贴在公共场所。一般由标题、正文、落款(或时间)三部分组成,在通知的正文上方用 Notice 或 Notification 作为标题。通知用第三人称,无称呼语。

如:

NOTICE

All teachers and students are requested to meet in the department conference room on Tuesday (May 21) at 2:30 p.m. to hear a report on Computer Assisted Language Learning.

The English Department Office
May 12, 2006

通　知

全体师生于 5 月 21 日星期二下午 2:30 在系会议室,听"计算机辅助语言学习"的报告。

英语系办公室
2006.5.12

Useful Expressions

Notice is hereby given that...
This is to announce that...

Exercises

I. Fill in the blanks in the following English Notice so that it is functionally equivalent to the Chinese version.

> **通 知**
>
> 请本系全体学生于本月 18 日星期三下午 5:30 在学校礼堂听"职业生涯设计"的讲座。
>
> 中文系办公室
> 2006.5.12

> **NOTICE**
>
> All students _____ meet in the auditorium _____, May 18, to hear a lecture on Career Design.
>
> The Chinese Department Office
> May 12, 2006

II. Write a Notice to inform all the teachers and students to attend its annual meeting in the department conference room on Monday (April 12) at 3:00 p.m.

Part V English Salon

English Poem

The Road Not Taken
by Robert Frost

Two roads diverged in a yellow wood,
And sorry I could not travel both
And be one traveler, long I stood
And looked down one as far as I could
To where it bent in the undergrowth;

...

I shall be telling this with a sigh
Somewhere ages and ages hence:
Two roads diverged in a wood, and I —
I took the one less traveled by,
And that has made all the difference.

Requirement

Read the poem and put it into Chinese.

Unit Seven

Part I Text

Guide to Text-Learning

1. Theme of the Text

One of Australia's most remarkable natural gifts, the Great Barrier Reef is blessed with the breathtaking beauty of the world's largest coral reef. The reef contains an abundance of marine life and comprises of over 3,000 individual reef systems and coral cays and literally hundreds of picturesque tropical islands with some of the worlds most beautiful sun-soaked, golden beaches.

2. Words and Expressions Related to the Topic

wonder	奇观, 奇迹
ecosystem	生态系统
the Ice Age	冰川时期
diversity	多样性
coral reef	珊瑚礁
patch reef	(珊瑚)礁坪
wall reef	壁礁
tropical rainforests	热带雨林
the Wet Tropics	昆士兰湿热带
tourist destination	旅游目的地
the Great Barrier Reef Marine Park	大堡礁海洋公园

3. Grammatical Structure to Learn

(1) The Great Barrier Reef system **consists of** more than 3,000 reefs.

大堡礁由3000多个珊瑚礁组成。

(2) Two main classes may be defined: platform or patch reefs, **resulting from** radial growth...

可以界定为两个主要类别：一是由径向生长而形成的平台珊瑚礁或礁坪……

(3) The Reef has over 600 islands which **are** easily **accessible** from North Queensland and coastal cities like Cairns and Port Douglas.

大堡礁的 600 多个岛屿交通便捷，从北昆士兰和沿海城市凯恩斯和道格拉斯港等前往均很方便。

4. Grammar

基本句型转换 II：祈使句（Imperative Sentence）

5. Practical English

Poster

Warming-Up Questions:

1. What is the only living thing on earth visible from space?
2. What is the reason for it to be listed in the World Natural Heritage?
3. What do you imagine can be found on the Great Barrier Reef?

The Great Barrier Reef

1 The Great Barrier Reef is the only living organic **collective** visible from Earth's **orbit**. The Great Barrier Reef, off the east coast of Australia, is one of the wonders of the natural world—it is the world's largest coral reef ecosystem.

2 Experts believe the Great Barrier Reef was formed around 18 million years ago. Due to various climatic and environmental changes,

collective /kəˈlektɪv/ *n.*
集体
orbit /ˈɔːbɪt/ *n.*
the (usually elliptical) path described by one celestial body in its revolution about another
轨道

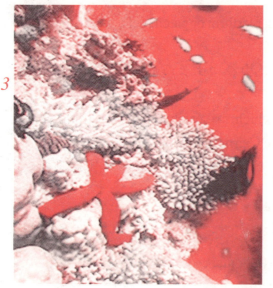

3   the reefs, which we see today, are those that have grown over the earlier reefs since the last Ice Age.

    The reef is **scattered** with beautiful islands and **idyllic** coral cays and covers more than 344,400 square kilometers. The Great Barrier Reef system consists of more than 3,000 reefs which range in size from 1 hectare to over 10,000 **hectares**. Dunk Island is one of more than 600 islands of the Great Barrier Reef.

4   The form and structure of the individual reefs show great variety. Two main classes may be defined: platform or patch reefs, resulting from radial growth; and wall reefs, resulting from elongated growth, often in areas of strong water currents. There are also many fringing reefs where the reef growth is established on subtidal rock of the mainland coast or continental islands.

5   The Great Barrier Reef is home to a wide diversity of life and beauty on the north-eastern coast of Australia. Studies have **revealed** it contains the world's largest collection of coral reefs, with some 400 types of coral, 1,500 species of fish and 4,000 types of mollusc. It is an area of great scientific value and also provides a **habitat** for many endangered species such as green turtle and dugong. As compared to any other location around the globe, an amazing fact about the Great Barrier Reef is that every **cubic** meter has many different species of animals and plants! And this itself explains the wide **diversity** of life.

6   One of the oldest species of fish that can

---

scatter /'skætə/ v.
strew or distribute over an area
散开,散播

idyllic /ai'dilik/ adj.
charmingly simple and serene
田园诗的

hectare /'hektɑː/ n.
a unit of surface area equal to 10,000 square meters
公顷

reveal /ri'viːl/ vt.
make clear and visible; display
显示,透露

habitat /'hæbitæt/ n.
environment in which an organism or group normally lives or occurs
(动植物的)生活环境,产地,栖息地

cubic /'kjuːbik/ adj.
having three dimensions
立方的

diversity /dai'vəːsiti/ n.
variety
差异,多样性

be found at the Great Barrier Reef is the Red Bass. This fish can live for more than 50 years as compared to other species. Some of the largest of giant clams can be found out here. One of the largest pearl was found in such a clam and was reportedly sold in New York for $10 million!

7   Although the reef stretches more than 2000 kilometers **offshore** from Queensland, it is only at Cape Tribulation, just north of Port Douglas that the reef comes right to the shore and meets the **tropical** rainforests of the Wet Tropics. The Reef has over 600 islands which are easily **accessible** from North Queensland and coastal cities like Cairns and Port Douglas. In 2006 there were approximately 820 operators and 1,500 **vessels** and aircraft permitted to operate in the Great Barrier Reef **Marine** Park providing ease of access for all to experience the Great Barrier Reef and learn first hand about its natural delights and World Heritage values.

8   Because of its natural beauty, both below and above the water's surface, the Great Barrier Reef has become one of the world's most sought-after tourist destinations. And UNESCO listed the Great Barrier Reef as a World Heritage Site in 1981.

(526 words)

offshore /'ɔːʃʃɔ/ adv.
away from land
离岸地
tropical /'trɔpikl/ adj.
of or relating to the tropics
热带的
accessible /ək'sesəbl/ adj.
capable of being reached
可进入的
vessel /'vesl/ n.
a ship or large boat
船;舰
marine /mə'riːn/ adj.
of or relating to the sea
海的,海生的

Useful Phrases ▶▶▶ ▶▶▶

be home to		是……的所在地,是……的家园
compared to		与……相比
range from... to		在……和……之间(变动)
consist of	be composed of	包含;由……组成
accessible from/to	capable of being reached from/to	可进入的
first hand	direct	直接的;第一手的
sought-after	being searched for or very popular	很吃香的,很受欢迎的

Notes

1 Due to various climatic and environmental changes, the reefs, which we see today, are those that have grown over the earlier reefs since the last Ice Age. 由于各种气候和环境变化，我们今天所看到的珊瑚礁是那些自冰河时期末期生成的珊瑚礁上不断堆积的结果。

"Due to" means "because of" or "owing to" when it is used as a prepositional phrase, but it also can function as an adjective phrase, meaning "be scheduled to"; for example:

The board is due to meet on Sunday. 董事会会议定于周日举行。

the Ice Age: 具有强烈冰川作用的地史时期。又称冰川期。

冰期有广义和狭义之分，广义的冰期又称大冰期，狭义的冰期是指比大冰期低一层次的冰期。大冰期是指地球上气候寒冷，极地冰盖增厚、广布，中、低纬度地区有时也有强烈冰川作用的地质时期。大冰期中气候较寒冷的时期称冰期，较温暖的时期称间冰期。大冰期、冰期和间冰期都是依据气候划分的地质时间单位。

2 As compared to any other location around the globe, an amazing fact about the Great Barrier Reef is that every cubic meter has many different species of animals and plants! And this itself explains the wide diversity of life. 与全球其他地方相比，大堡礁每立方米含有许多不同种类的动物和植物，这一事实令人称奇，其本身说明了生命的多样性！

连词 as 与过去分词短语 compared to... 一起在句中充当时间状语。

3 Although the reef stretches more than 2000 kilometers offshore from Queensland, it is only at Cape Tribulation, just north of Port Douglas that the reef comes right to the shore and meets the tropical rainforests of the Wet Tropics. 大堡礁沿昆士兰州海岸绵延 2000 余公里，仅从道格拉斯港以北的考验角折向海岸，与昆士兰湿热带地区的热带雨林相接。

Cape Tribulation 考验角，位于道格拉斯港以北。作为一个海角，最为独特的是，这里是大堡礁和热带雨林合二为一的地方，因此是户外运动爱好者的天堂。

The Wet Tropics 昆士兰的湿热地带是少有的几个满足所有 4 个世

界自然遗产名录条件的地区之一,它展现了地球上生物进化历史过程的主要阶段,是一个突出表现正在进行的生态与生物进程的实例,包含最高级的自然现象,是最重要的保有自然生物多样性的生物栖息地。

4. Red Bass, a kind of fish 红鲈鱼

Reading Aloud and Memorizing

I. Read the following paragraph taken from the text until you learn it by heart.

Although the reef stretches more than 2000 kilometers offshore from Queensland, it is only at Cape Tribulation, just north of Port Douglas that the reef comes right to the shore and meets the tropical rainforests of the Wet Tropics. The Reef has over 1000 islands which are easily accessible from North Queensland and coastal cities like Cairns and Port Douglas. The coral islands are very popular tourist attractions. Some even have varied vegetation including rainforest and are encircled by the coral reefs.

Comprehension of the text

II. Choose the best answer to each of the following questions according to the passage.

1. According to the passage, which of the following statements is right?
   A. The Great Barrier Reef is one of the living things visible from Earth's orbit.
   B. The Great Barrier Reef is the only living thing visible from Earth's orbit.
   C. The Great Barrier Reef is the only living organic thing that can be seen from Earth's orbit.
   D. The Great Barrier Reef is visible from the moon.

2. The Great Barrier Reef is believed to come into being _____ million years ago.
   A. 12   B. 14   C. 16   D. 18
3. The amazing difference of the Great Barrier Reef from other places in the world is _____.
   A. red bass   B. variety of life   C. sharks   D. largest pearl
4. The only point of the Reef that is connected with the land is _____.
   A. Cape Tribulation   B. Cairns   C. Sydney   D. Queensland
5. All the following can be catalogued into marine life except _____.
   A. sea turtle   B. whale   C. coral   D. rainforest

III. Answer the following questions with the information you've got from the text.

1. Where does the Great Barrier Reef lie?   (Para.1)
2. How many classes of reefs can be found and what are they?   (Para. 4)
3. Can you explain the wide diversity of life on the Great Barrier Reef?   (Para. 5)
4. What is the special characteristic of the Red Bass at the Great Barrier Reef?   (Para. 8)
5. What size is the Great Barrier Reef?   (Para. 3)

Vocabulary

IV. Find the definition in column B which matches the words or expressions in column A.

A	B
1. diversity	( ) a. display
2. accessible	( ) b. distribute
3. scatter	( ) c. variety
4. reveal	( ) d. capable of being reached
5. offshore	( ) e. able to be seen
6. marine	( ) f. away from land
7. vegetation	( ) g. of or relating to the sea
8. catalogue	( ) h. classify
9. visible	( ) i. direct
10. first hand	( ) j. all the plant life in a particular place or period

V. Fill in the blanks with the words given in the brackets. Change the form where necessary.

1. They are the people from _____ cultures. (diversity)
2. Citizens may have free _____ to the library. (accessible)
3. Pulses are a good source of protein for _____. (vegetation)
4. The gallery produced a _____ of young artists. (catalogue)
5. She selected a diamond ring from the _____. (collective)
6. Different _____ is having different design to ask to the use function of the bedroom. (habitat)
7. The starchy root of any of these plants, is used in the _____ as food. (tropical)
8. There's a lot of talk about putting up manned _____ stations. (orbit)
9. _____ showers are expected this afternoon. (scatter)
10. There are more than 50 _____ on this ship. (marine)

VI. Complete each of the following sentences with the most appropriate word or words from the four choices. Marked A, B, C and D.

1. You will find the post office just _____ High Street.
   A. off   B. of   C. away   D. far
2. Sentences today range _____ 5 or 6 words _____ 70, with the majority not far from 20.
   A. in, of   B. from, or   C. on, in   D. from, to
3. Life is poetically compared _____ the morning dew.
   A. with   B. to   C. for   D. of
4. The shore was barely _____ through the fog.
   A. see   B. visibleness C. visible   D. visibly
5. These few words fully _____ her noble quality.
   A. review   B. revealed   C. reform   D. reserve
6. If the team makes a strong _____ effort, we'll win the game.
   A. collect   B. collection C. collective   D. collectively
7. These Games were monumentally important to the host nation, which happens to _____ 1/5 of humanity.
   A. be home to   B. be   C. have   D. come

8. I like watching TV _____ to the cinema.
   A. more than to go   B. more than going
   C. than going   D. rather than to go

9. Our journey was slow because the train stopped _____ at different villages.
   A. continually   B. continuously   C. gradually   D. unceasingly

10. Don't get your schedule _____, stay with us in this class.
    A. to change   B. changed   C. changing   D. change

Structure

VII. Rewrite the following sentences after the models.

Model 1   The Great Barrier Reef system is made up of more than 3,000 reefs.
           The Great Barrier Reef system **consists of** more than 3,000 reefs.

1. The exam is composed of two parts: a written test and an oral.
2. The group is made up of senior people from education and business.
3. His job consists of answering the phone and making coffee.
4. The committee was composed entirely of specialists.
5. The United Kingdom is made up of Great Britain and Northern Ireland.

Model 2   Two main classes may be defined: platform or patch reefs, following as the consequence of radial growth; and wall reefs...
           Two main classes may be defined: platform or patch reefs, **resulting from** radial growth; and wall reefs...

1. Nothing had occurred as the effect of our efforts.
2. His failure was the consequence of not working hard enough.
3. Great dangers can be the consequence of misconceiving of the enemy's intentions.
4. Earthquake can be caused by stress in the earth's crust.
5. The increase in debt was caused by the expansion programme.

III. Study the model and translate the following sentences into English.

Model The Reef has over 600 islands which **are** easily **accessible** from North Queensland and coastal cities like Cairns and Port Douglas.

1. 他比大多数大亨都要平易近人。
2. 只有授权的管理员才可以访问此数据库。
3. 资料应该明白易懂。
4. 这个小岛只能坐小船去。
5. 一个管理人员应该让职员感到平易近人。

IX. Translate the following sentences into Chinese.

1. The Great Barrier Reef is the world's largest coral reef ecosystem.

2. Experts believe the Great Barrier Reef was formed around 18 million years ago.

3. As compared to any other location around the globe, an amazing fact about the Great Barrier Reef is that every cubic meter has many different species of animals and plants!

4. One of the oldest species of fish that can be found at the Great Barrier Reef is the Red Bass.

5. Because of its natural beauty, both below and above the water's surface, the Great Barrier Reef has become one of the world's most sought-after tourist destinations.

X. Translate the following sentences into English using the words or phrases in the brackets.

1. 她站在昏暗的光线里,半隐半现。(visible)

2. 价格自五美元至十美元不等。(range from... to)

3. 生产商承受着维持产品多样化的压力。(diversity)

4. 他们被控引发了一起可能危及生命的爆炸事件。(endanger)

5. 教师的工作常被比作蜡烛。(compare)

Part II Grammar

基本句型转换 II

Imperative Sentences（祈使句）

祈使句是说话者向对方发出的请求、命令、叮嘱和号召等，主语通常为第二人称"you"，常省略，其谓语动词用原形。

Examples:

Go and wash your hands.	去洗手。
Be quiet, please. (Please be quiet.)	请安静。
Keep off the grass.	勿践草坪。

祈使句的否定形式在谓语动词前加 don't，也可由 never 引起。

Examples:

Don't let the dog in.	不要让那只狗进来。
Don't be silly.	别傻了。
Never make the same mistake again.	别再犯同样的错误了。

还可以用动词 let 引导一个祈使句，用以提出建议。

Examples:

Let me help you with it.	让我来帮助你吧。
Let's go for a walk.	咱们出去走走吧。
Let's not mention it any more.	咱们别再提这事了。
Let him (them) clean the room.	让他（他们）去打扫房间吧。

祈使句中如果有称呼语，要用逗号隔开，放在句首或句末。

Examples:

Come here, Dave.	大卫，你过来一下。
Mary, go to answer the door.	玛丽，去把门打开。

 **Exercises**

I. Complete each of the following sentences with the most appropriate word or words from the four choices marked A, B, C and D.

1. _____ take it up with the headmaster.
   A. Do   B. Let's   C. Have   D. Does
2. _____ out of here.
   A. Get   B. Got   C. Have gotten   D. Will get
3. _____ a cigarette.
   A. Have   B. Has   C. Do   D. Had
4. _____ your seat belt.
   A. Keep   B. Do   C. Fasten   D. Have
5. _____ it right away.
   A. Did   B. Will do   C. Do   D. Have done
6. Let's _____ say anything about it.
   A. don't   B. not   C. no   D. doesn't
7. _____ sure to get here before nine.
   A. You are   B. Be   C. Please   D. Do
8. _____ waste our time.
   A. Let's   B. Please   C. Let's not   D. Do
9. _____ do that again.
   A. No   B. Nor   C. Never   D. Either
10. _____ quiet.
    A. Will be   B. Are   C. Have   D. Be

II. Change the following into imperative sentences.

1. You are sure to turn off the lights before you leave the room.
2. You should take care not to lose your way.
3. We must grasp every minute to give them a reply.
4. You need not bother waiting for me for lunch.
5. You need not be so nervous, Tim.

III. Put the following imperative sentences into Chinese.

1. Do be patient!
2. Let's give a hand to him.
3. Let us help you.
4. Never put off till tomorrow what you can do today.
5. Study hard and you will get good result.

Part III Reading Practice

Guide to Reading

1. Words and Expressions to Learn

monument	n.	纪念碑
visible	adj.	看得见的
conquer	v.	征服
border	n.	国界, 边境
tribe	n.	部落
trace	n.	痕迹, 踪迹
inner	adj.	内部的, 里面的
the World Cultural Heritage		世界文化遗产
attribute to		归于, 归因于
conform to		符合, 遵照
in case of		假设, 万一
at regular intervals		每隔一定间隔
the Qin Dynasty		秦朝
the Ming Dynasty		明朝

2. Pre-Reading Questions

(1) Have you ever been to the Great Wall?
(2) Could you tell us the history of the Great Wall?

The Great Wall

1   The Great Wall is probably China's best-known monument and one of its most popular tourist attractions. In 1987 it was **designated** (*v.* 指派,指定) a World Cultural Heritage Site by the United Nations Educational, Scientific and Cultural Organization (UNESCO). The Great Wall is made up of a network of walls and towers, with an estimated length of about 6,400 km, or even longer.

2   The most famous early wall construction is attributed to the king of the Qin Dynasty, who conquered the other states and unified China in 221 BC. Taking the title of Shihuangdi, or First Emperor, Qin Shihuang ordered his soldiers to conquer the tribes of the north in order to strengthen the border. Few traces exist today of the ancient wall of Shihuangdi. Today's Great Wall consists of a series of walls built by the Ming Dynasty beginning in the late 15th century A.D. The Ming had suffered a military defeat by the **Mongols** (*n.* 蒙古人). To ensure the safety of the dynasty, the Ming rulers decided to keep the Mongols out by building walls along China's northern border. Unfortunately, the walls proved **ineffective** (*adj.* 无效的), as the Mongols were easily able to pass around or break through them during their attack.

3   Although the first Ming walls were built of earth in the traditional manner, by the 16th century the work had become much more **elaborate** (*adj.* 精心制作的,精细的) and was done in stone by professional builders. Bit by bit, in response to Mongol challenges, the Ming heavily reinforced the region around the capital at Beijing. Other areas were protected with shorter walls or **forts** (*n.* 堡垒).

4   Wall building and repairs continued until the Ming Dynasty fell to the Qing

Dynasty in 1644. By this time, the walls formed a complete and uneven network, with the eastern end at Qinhuangdao in Hebei Province on the Bohai **Gulf** (*n.* 海湾), while the western extreme near Jiayuguan in Gansu Province. They included inner walls and outer walls, and some **stretches** (*n.* 一段路程) had watchtowers placed at regular intervals so that alarm signals could be passed between them in case of attack. Along the top of the walls was space for soldiers to march. The walls around Beijing measured at least 7.6 m (25 ft) in height and up to 9 m (30 ft) in width, **tapering** (*v.* 逐步减少) from the base to the top.

5 As a cultural heritage, the Great Wall belongs not only to China but to the world. Today, the Wall has become a must-see for every visitor to China. Few can help saying "Wow!" when they stand on top of a beacon **tower** (*n.* 烽火台) and look at this giant dragon.

(479 words)

I. Answer the following questions according to the passage.

1. When did the United Nations Educational, Scientific and Cultural Organization (UNESCO) designate the Great Wall the World Cultural Heritage Site?
2. Why did the Ming Dynasty build the walls along the northern border?
3. The Ming Dynasty constructed the walls along China's northern border. But the walls proved ineffective, why?
4. When did professional builders begin to build the wall in stone?
5. What was the function of the watchtowers?

II. Translate into Chinese the following sentences taken from the passage.

1. The existing wall is not several thousand years old, nor is it, as has been widely claimed, visible with the naked eye from outer space.

2. Few traces exist today of the ancient wall of Shihuangdi. Today's Great Wall consists of a series of walls built by the Ming Dynasty beginning in the late 15th century A.D.
3. Although the first Ming walls were built of earth in the traditional manner, by the 16th century the work had become much more elaborate and was done in stone by professional builders.
4. The walls around Beijing measured at least 7.6 m in height and up to 9 m in width, tapering from the base to the top.
5. Today, the Wall has become a must-see for every visitor to China. Few can help saying "Wow!" when they stand on top of a beacon tower and look at this giant dragon.

III. Fill in the blanks with the words or phrases listed in Words and Expressions to Learn. Change the form where necessary.

1. The criminal escaped over the _____ .
2. They searched the building but did not find any _____ of the criminal.
3. He gave me a number to call _____ emergency.
4. The smoke from the fire was _____ from the road.
5. They arranged the chairs around the room _____ .
6. Modern medical science _____ many diseases.
7. David _____ his company's success _____ the unity of all the staff and their persevering hard work.
8. Can you see the _____ meaning of this poem?

IV. Complete the following sentences.

1. The family _____ (追溯到) its history to the 17th century.
2. Millions of people gave freely _____ (响应) the famine appeal.
3. If you want to _____ (确保) that you catch the plane, take a taxi.
4. You should _____ (不卷入) these things.
5. He comes back to see us _____ (每隔一段时间).

Part IV Practical English

Poster（海报）

海报是具有宣布性质的张贴通告,是广告的一种。主要用于单位或个人告知他人诸如影视戏剧、体育赛事、学术报告、节目预告以及参观游览等信息。

海报通常涉及主办单位、活动形式与内容、议程安排、时间和地点及参加方式等内容。

如:

> **The Student Union**
> **Of the English Department**
> Takes pleasure in inviting you to
> Its Annual English Speech Contest
> To be held
> In the department conference room
> On Friday evening, May 10, 2009 at 7 p.m.

> **英语系学生会**
> 诚邀各位参加于 2009 年 5 月 10 日
> 星期五下午 7 时在系会议室举办的一年一度的
> 英语演讲比赛

I. Fill in the blanks in the following English poster so that it is functionally equivalent to the Chinese version.

讲　座

　　由外国文学研究会主办，美国密尔顿教授将于 2009 年 4 月 20 日下午两点半在图书馆阅览室举办当代英国文学讲座。欢迎参加。

外国文学研究会办公室
2009.4.12

Lecture

All are warmly welcome
Under the auspices of the Foreign Literature Society
A lecture _____ on Contemporary Literature
By visiting American Prof. Milton
In the _____
On April 20, 2009
At 2:30 p.m.

The Society Office
April 12, 2009

II. Write a poster on friendly basketball match with the information below.

Women Basketball Match
National Team vs. US Team
Time: 3:00 p.m., Aug.16
Place: Municipal Gymnasium

Part V   English Salon

Humorous Story

A Good Idea

When the office printer's type began to grow faint, the office manager called a local repair shop where a friendly service agent told him that the printer probably only needed a thorough cleaning. Because the store charged $50 for such cleanings, he said, the manager might try reading the printer's manual and doing the job himself.

Pleasantly surprised by the man's candor, the office manager asked, "Does your boss know that you discourage business?"

"Actually it's my boss's idea," the employee replied. "We usually make more money on repairs if we let people try to fix things themselves first."

Requirement

Retell the story in your own words.

Unit Eight

Part I Text

Guide to Text-Learning

1. Theme of the Text

  Beautiful natural scenery and wild animals are the great attractions to people today. This unit will provide you with the knowledge of geological feature in a natural park and wild animal life in a nature reserve. So how to preserve these nature heritages is the big issue all of us have to face with now.

2. Words and Expressions related to the topic

flagship	旗舰
geyser	间歇泉
hydrothermal	热水的，热液的
geothermal attraction	地热景观
ecosystem	生态系统
petrified trees	石化树
temperate zone	温带

3. Grammatical Structures to Learn

 (1) Yellowstone National Park **is a favorite** to millions of visitors each year.
   每年成千上万的人特别喜欢到黄石国家公园旅游。

 (2) The human history of the park is evidenced by cultural sites **dating back** 12,000 years.
   公园的文化遗址证明这里的人类历史始于 12,000 年前。

 (3) **Contrary to** popular belief Old Faithful is not the largest geyser in the park.

大家都认为老忠实泉是公园里最大的间歇泉,其实并非如此。

4. Grammar

基本句型转换 III:Exclamatory Sentence:1. what 引导的感叹句;2. how 引导的感叹句

5. Practical English

Notices

Warming-Up Questions:

1. Have you heard anything about Yellowstone National Park?
2. Where is Yellowstone National Park located?
3. What are the special features of the park?

Yellowstone National Park

—— The World's First National Park

1 Yellowstone National Park is a favorite to millions of visitors each year, the flagship of the National Park Service in the world. Since the first explorers began **documenting** their discoveries in modern day, the features of Yellowstone National Park have in fact remained the same.

2 Yellowstone was the first national park created by the US government in 1876 to **preserve** the natural beauty of this strange and beautiful place. In addition to preserving its various geothermal attractions, Yellowstone National Park serves as a good place for a wide variety of American native wildlife. The last remaining herd of wild buffalo in the USA still peacefully wanders on the

---

document /ˈdɔkjumənt/ v.
support with evidence
证明

preserve /priˈzəːv/ v.
maintain in safety from injury; protect
保护

meadows of Yellowstone. You can easily **spot** many of these wild animals such as deer, eagles, bears and wolves from your car as you drive through the **magnificent scenery** of Yellowstone.

3   The features that at first attracted interest, and led to the preservation of Yellowstone as a national park, were geological: the geothermal **phenomena** (there are more geysers and hot springs here than in the rest of the world combined), the colorful Grand Canyon of the Yellowstone River, **fossil** forests, and the Yellowstone Lake. The human history of the park is evidenced by cultural sites dating back 12,000 years. More recent history can be seen in the historic structures and sites that represent the various periods of park administration and visitor facilities development.

4   Old Faithful, the famous geyser, is the most popular attraction of Yellowstone National Park. It erupts more frequently than other large geysers. Contrary to popular belief Old Faithful is not the largest geyser in the park. Eruptions at Old Faithful last from 1 to 5 minutes, and **spray** water and steam up to 184 feet, at intervals of every 80 minutes.

5   The interest in seeing a **wolf** has become one of the main wildlife attractions for visitors coming to Yellowstone from both around the country and the world. It's not unusual most days in the park to see a crowd gather along roadsides in hopes of glimpsing one of the **rare** wild animals. Visitors planning to visit the park to see wolves or Yellowstone's other typical wildlife are reminded

---

meadow /'medəu/ n.
grassland
草地,牧场

spot /spɒt/ v.
detect or discern, especially visually
辨认,认出

magnificent /mæg'nifisənt/ adj.
splendid; grand
壮观的,宏伟的

scenery /'siːnəri/ n.
a view or views of natural features
风景

phenomenon /fi'nɔminən/ n.
sth that happens or exists
现象

fossil /'fɒsl/ n.
the remains, on a mark, of a prehistoric animal or plant that has been buried in rock for a very long time and that has become hard
化石

spray /sprei/ v.
scatter in the form of tiny particles
喷射,喷溅

wolf /wulf/ n.
a wide animal that looks like a dog and that lives and hunts in a group
狼

rare /rɛə/ adj.
uncommon
罕见的,稀有的

to be very careful and remember that the animals are wild.

6   Yellowstone National Park forms the **core** of the Greater Yellowstone Ecosystem (GYE) — one of the largest untouched temperate zone ecosystems on the earth today. This 28,000-square-mile **region** preserves and feeds a variety of wildlife species and the natural processes that keep them alive.

7   Each of Yellowstone National Park's separate parts—the hydrothermal features, the wildlife, the lakes, the Grand Canyon of the Yellowstone River, and the **petrified** trees—could easily stand alone as a principle element of a national park. They are all at one place, which is **evidence** of Greater Yellowstone's variety and natural wealth.

core /kɔː/ n.		
the central or innermost part		
中心,核心		
region /ˈriːdʒən/ n.		
a large area of land		
地区,区域		
petrify /ˈpetriˌfai/ v.		
convert into a stony replica by petrifaction		
石化		
evidence /ˈevidəns/ n.		
proof		
证明,证实;证据,迹象		

Useful Phrases ▶▶▶   ▶▶▶

in addition to	besides	加于……之上;除……之外又
serve as	be of service or use; function	用于,当作
a variety of	a number of (varied things)	种种,各类
herd of	a number of wild animals	兽群,牧群
date back		回溯至
contrary to	in an opposite direction or manner	方向或行为上相反地;反方向地
at intervals of		相隔,每隔

Proper Names

Yellowstone National Park 黄石国家公园
Old Faithful 老忠实泉
Grand Canyon （美国）大峡谷

Notes

1. The last remaining herd of wild buffalo in the USA still peacefully wanders on the meadows of Yellowstone. 美国残存的最后一批野牛依然安静地在公园草地上漫步。

2. More recent history can be seen in the historic structures and sites that represent the various periods of park administration and visitor facilities development. 公园的历史建筑和遗址是近代史的见证，它们代表了不同时期的公园管理和旅游设施的发展。
   that represent the various period 是定语从句，修饰 the historic structures and site。

3. It's not unusual most days in the park to see a crowd gather along roadsides in hopes of glimpsing one of the rare wild animals. 在公园里经常可以看见人们聚集在道路旁，期望能目睹珍稀野生动物。
   It's not unusual 是双重否定结构，表示肯定，有强调的意味。又如：
   At major athletic events, it is not uncommon to find 90,000 or 100,000 people sitting in the stands. 在一些重大体育赛事中，往往有9万或10万人坐在看台上。

Exercises

Reading Aloud and Memorizing the Following

I. Read the following paragraph taken from the text until you learn it by heart.

The features that at first attracted interest, and led to the preservation of Yellowstone as a national park, were geological: the geothermal phenomena (there are more geysers and hot springs here than in the rest of the world combined), the colorful Grand Canyon of the Yellowstone River, fossil forests, and the Yellowstone Lake. The human history of the park is evidenced by cultural sites dating back 12,000 years. More recent history can be seen in the historic structures and sites that represent the various periods of park administration and visitor facilities development.

Comprehension of the Text

II. Choose the best answer to each of the following questions according to the passage.

1. Yellowstone National Park attracts millions of visitors because of _____.
   A. its largest size in the world
   B. the first explorers documenting their discoveries to now
   C. its geothermal attractions and natural beauty
   D. its name having remained the same

2. Yellowstone National Park is a favorite to millions of visitors each year, the flagship of the National Park Service in the world. Here the word "flagship" means _____.
   A. a ship with flags   B. a flag post
   C. a name of a ship   D. the chief one of a related group

3. The typical features of the park are _____.
   A. geologies   B. wild animals
   C. human histories   D. visitor facilities

4. The name of "Old Faithful" means that _____.
   A. it exists a very long time   B. it always erupts at the same interval
   C. it is very reliable   D. it is the largest geyser
5. Which of the following is not mentioned in the text?
   A. The Grand Canyon.   B. The geothermal phenomena.
   C. The wild life.   D. The rocky mountains.

III. Answer the following questions with the information you've got from the text.

1. Why are there vast herds of wild animals in the Yellowstone National Park? (Para. 2)
2. What are the typical features of the park? (Para. 3)
3. Why is Old faithful the most popular attraction of the park? (Para. 4)
4. Why do we say Yellowstone National Park forms the core of the Greater Yellowstone Ecosystem? (Para. 6)
5. Can you list the most famous parts of the park? (Para. 7)

Vocabulary

IV. Find the definition in column B which matches the words or expressions in column A.

A	B
1. core	(　) a. the chief ship
2. date back	(　) b. characteristic
3. flagship	(　) c. protect
4. feature	(　) d. besides
5. preserve	(　) e. uncommon
6. contrary to	(　) f. central part
7. represent	(　) g. proof
8. evidence	(　) h. have lasted since the date of
9. rare	(　) i. completely different
10. in addition to	(　) j. stand for

153

V. Fill in the blanks with the words given in the brackets. Change the form where necessary.

1. I hope you will give _____ consideration to my suggestion. (favor)
2. I will go ahead with three of you, and the _____ can wait here. (remain)
3. It's _____ at home when the children are at school. (peace)
4. The idea of working for state-owned enterprises has little _____ to young people nowadays. (attract)
5. The railway _____ to these small villages is no longer economic. (serve)
6. This play is divided into three acts, and each act has three _____. (scenery)
7. They were pleased to meet after such a long _____. (separate)
8. The people _____ into the elevator. (crowd)
9. Mr Thompson gave all the _____ papers of his grandfather to the public library according to his grandfather's will. (history)
10. Rains are _____ here in early summer. (frequent)

VI. Complete each of the following sentences with the most appropriate word or words from the four choices marked A, B, C, and D.

1. David's a great favourite _____ his teacher.
   A. to   B. with   C. of   D. in
2. Stephen has served _____ the U.S. Air Force for ten years.
   A. in   B. as   C. for   D. to
3. _____ gene, intelligence also depends on an adequate diet, a good education and a decent home environment.
   A. Except   B. Beside   C. In addition   D. In addition to
4. The shopping-centre sells a _____ of goods.
   A. kind   B. variety   C. sort   D. type
5. This dance is _____ with young people.
   A. dear   B. common   C. popular   D. ordinary
6. The main _____ was a Charlie Chaplin film.
   A. attraction   B. attracting   C. attracted   D. attracts
7. Can you show me any evidence _____ your statement?
   A. as   B. of   C. for   D. on

8. He gave all his _____ papers to the library.
   A. history　　　　B. historical　　　　C. historic　　　　D. historian
9. I'm not sick; _____, I'm in the peak of health.
   A. on the contrary　　　　　　　B. in the contrary
   C. for the contrary　　　　　　　D. contrary to
10. This reminds me _____ my college days.
    A. to　　　　B. of　　　　C. for　　　　D. on

Structure

VII. Rewrite the following sentences after the models.

Model 1　Mr. Smith likes him very much.
　　　　　　He is **a favorite of** Mr. Smith's.

1. The teacher likes the serious student.
2. What was the subject she likes best in lessons?
3. A teacher shouldn't have preference in the class.
4. Is this the song you prefer?
5. The Summer Palace attracts thousands of visitors every year.

Model 2　This statue was carved in 500 B.C.
　　　　　　This statue **dates back** to 500 B.C.

1. This town was built in Roman times.
2. The connection with Hanover started from the 18th century.
3. These societies began as far as a century ago.
4. The castle has existed since the 14th century.
5. The scientists found the existing time of the fossil after much study.

VIII. Study the model and translate the following sentences into English.

Model　　He passed the examination, **contrary to** what I expected.

1. 他的意见和我相反。
2. 你想做的事是违反规章制度的。
3. 这与她通常的习惯完全相反。

4. 同我想的情况相反,他已经证明他成功了。

5. 他不听任何劝告,放弃了工作,去了南方。

Translation

IX. Translate the following sentences into Chinese.

1. Since the first explorers began documenting their discoveries to modern day, the features of Yellowstone National Park have in fact remained the same.

2. In addition to preserving its various geothermal attractions, Yellowstone National Park serves as a good place for a wide variety of American native wildlife.

3. You can easily spot many of these wild animals such as deer, eagles, bears and wolves from your car as you drive through the magnificent scenery of Yellowstone.

4. Old Faithful, the famous geyser, is the most popular attraction of Yellowstone National Park.

5. The interest in seeing a wolf has become one of the main wildlife attractions for visitors coming to Yellowstone from both around the country and the world.

X. Translate the following sentences into English using the words or phrases in the brackets.

1. 博物馆藏有几幅代表这个艺术家早期风格的油画。(represent)

2. 她的住房亦作办公室使用。(serve as)

3. 我们必须保护自然资源。(preserve)

4. 山里的景色非常美。(scenery)

5. 黄石国家公园里有各种各样的野生动物。(a variety of)

Part II Grammar

基本句型转换Ⅲ

Exclamatory Sentences（感叹句）

感叹句一般是用来表示说话时的喜悦、惊讶等情感。英语感叹句常用 what 和 how 引导，what 和 how 与所修饰的词置于句首，其他部分用陈述句语序。

一、由 what 引导的感叹句：what 意为"多么"，用作定语，修饰名词，名词前可有其他定语成分（即：形容词或冠词）。单数可数名词前要加不定冠词 a/an，复数可数名词或不可数名词前不用冠词。结构主要有以下几种：

What + a + 形容词+名词+陈述语序	What a stupid man (he is)!
What + 形容词+复数名词+陈述语序	What beautiful flowers (we have)!
What + 形容词+不可数名词+陈述语序	What delicious food it is!
What + 名词 + 陈述语序	What noise they are making!

二、由 how 引导的感叹句：how 意为"多么"，用作状语，修饰形容词或副词。如果修饰形容词，则句中的谓语动词用系动词；如果 how 修饰副词，则句中的谓语动词用行为动词，这类句子的结构形式是：

How +形容词+a+名词+陈述语序	How stupid a man he is!
How +形容词+陈述语序	How beautiful the flowers are!
How +副词+ 陈述语序	How fast the boy was running!

三、感叹句在表示激动的感情时，口语中常常采用省略句，后面的主语和谓语往往略去。

What a fine day!　　多么晴的天呀！
How cool!　　好凉快呀！

Exercises

I. Choose the best answer.

1. _____ food you've cooked!
   A. How a nice   B. What a nice   C. How nice   D. What nice
2. _____ terrible weather we've been having these days!
   A. What a   B. What   C. How   D. How a
3. —— _____ I had!
   —— You really suffered a lot.
   A. What a time   B. What time   C. How a time   D. How time
4. _____ well you look!
   A. What   B. What a   C. How   D. How a
5. _____ of you to have done me such a favour!
   A. What a nice   B. What nice   C. How nice a   D. How nice

II. Change the following sentences into exclamatory sentences.

1. Yellowstone was a very strange and beautiful place.
2. Old Faithful is the most popular attraction of Yellowstone National Park.
3. You can easily spot many of these wild animals in Yellowstone.
4. The Wolong Nature Reserve is very rich in other mammals, birds and reptiles.
5. You can be as flexible with your time as you like.

III. Change the following sentences into exclamatory sentences according to the requirement:

1. It is quite a nice present. → _____ _____ nice present!
2. We have fine weather today. → _____ _____ weather we have today!
3. It's sunny today. → _____ _____ sunny day it is today!
4. The children are working hard. → _____ _____ the children are working!
5. She played basketball wonderfully. → _____ _____ she played basketball!
6. He is good at singing. → _____ _____ he sings!

7. He was doing well in dancing.→ _____ a _____ dancer he was!
8. Tom coughs badly.→ _____ _____ _____ cough Tom has!
9. The fish is very lovely.→ _____ _____ the fish is!
10. They live a happy life today.→ _____ _____ _____ life they live!

Part III Reading Practice

Guide to Reading

1. Words and Expressions to Learn

focus	v.	使集中于焦点,集中
artificial	adj.	人工的;人为的
breeding	n.	饲养
release	vt.	释放
adapt	v.	适应
classify	vt.	分类,分等
maturity	n.	成熟,完全发育
ecology	n.	生态学
accommodation	n.	住处;膳宿
biosphere	n.	生物圈
fauna	n.	动物群,动物区系,动物志
abound in		富于
UNESCO		联合国教科文组织
captive cage		圈地
semi-nature enclosure		半自然圈养
endow with		赋予
as well as		也,又

2. Pre-Reading Questions

(1) What do you know about nature reserve in China?

(2) Where and when did you see pandas?

Wolong Nature Reserve

1   The Wolong Nature **Reserve** (*n.* 保护区), or sometimes known as "Wolong Giant Panda Reserve," is probably the most important and the largest giant panda reserve in China as well as in the world, situated in the heart of the giant panda range at an **elevation** (*n.* 海拔) of 6,500 feet (1,980 m), about 120km (74 miles) northwest of Chengdu in Wenchuan County of Sichuan Province.

2   Today, the Wolong Giant Panda Reserve Center has been turned into the Giant Panda Breeding Center focusing mainly on continuing studies of artificial breeding in the hopes that they may successfully achieve live births of giant pandas which, after the panda baby reaches maturity, will be released into the forests.  The other primary function of the reserve is **bamboo** (*n.* 竹子) ecology.

3   The Wolong Giant Panda Reserve Center offers two types of accommodations for the giant pandas:

4   1. Captive Cages:

5   Most of the giant pandas stay individually in the captive cages. They are simply large enclosures, each consisting of an indoor room and an outdoor courtyard.

6   2. Semi-Nature Enclosures:

7   The semi-nature enclosures are very large wild areas but protected by border fences. Giant pandas that will soon be released back to the wild will be put in the semi-nature enclosures for a period of time **sufficient** (*adj.* 足够的) enough for them to adapt to the natural environment. Although food still has to be provided, the giant pandas will sleep there, eat there and recover their natural survival skills until they can be safely released back into the wild.

8   The Wolong Nature Reserve is also rich in other wild animals and birds. Apart from the panda, the 46 kinds of wild animals living in Wolong include the **takin** (*n.* [动]羚牛), the **golden snub-nosed monkey** ([动]金丝猴), the white-lipped deer and the clouded leopard, all of which are classified Level 1 for state protection. The 225 bird species include a number of rare **pheasants** (*n.* [动]野鸡) which are probably dependent on the panda reserves for their survival.

9   The UN has declared Wolong an international biosphere preserve and in addition to the wealth of fauna, 4,000 different types of plants are believed to grow here, including 667 hectares of rare **dove tree** ([植] 珙桐) forest, **Japanese larch** ([植]日本落叶松), the U.S pine, **spruce** (*n.* [植]云杉) etc. It abounds in bamboos which are the favorite feed of the grand panda.

10   The Wolong Nature Reserve is also a world of flowers. Fifteen types of azalea (*n.* [植]杜鹃花) have been discovered. In autumn, different kinds of blossoms and tree leaves of various colors decorate the mountains and forests like a series of brilliant and colorful paintings.

11   It was admitted by the UNESCO to be part of "the International Reserve Net of Man and Biosphere." Lying on the complicated land formations of **transition area**(*n.* 过渡地带) from the **Qinghai and Tibet Plateau**(青藏高原) to the **Sichuan Basin** (四川盆地), and with a cool climate, it's endowed with favorable conditions for the preservation and reproduction of a number of living beings.

Exercises

Reading Comprehension

I. Answer the following questions according to the passage.

1. Where is the Wolong Nature Reserve located?
2. What is the main purpose of establishing the Wolong Nature Reserve?
3. How many types of accommodation does the Reserve Centre offer for the giant panda? What are they?
4. How many kinds of wild animals besides giant pandas are there in the park?
5. Why did UNESO admit Wolong to be part of "the International Reserve Net of Man and Biosphere"?

II. Translate into Chinese the following sentences taken from the passage.

1. The Wolong Nature Reserve, or sometimes known as "Wolong Giant Panda Reserve," is probably the most important and the largest giant panda reserve in China as well as in the world.
2. The semi-nature enclosures are very large wild areas but protected by border fences.
3. The Wolong Nature Reserve is also rich in other wild animals and birds.
4. In autumn, different kinds of blossoms and tree leaves of various colors decorate the mountains and forests like a series of brilliant and colorful paintings.
5. It was admitted by the UNESCO to be part of "the International Reserve Net of Man and Biosphere."

III. Fill in the blanks with the words or phrases listed in the Words and Expressions to Learn. Change the form where necessary.

1. The new dam will form a large _____ lake behind it.
2. Cattle _____ is a big business.
3. To _____ a prisoner is to set him free.

4. He has not yet _____ to the climate.

5. Wild animals _____ the park.

6. Few men _____ the brain of an Einstein.

7. In the post-office mail _____ according to the places where it is to go.

8. It is important for you _____ for me.

IV. Complete the following sentences.

1. You should _____ (集中注意力) on your work.

2. _____ (很少有人具有) the brain of an Einstein.

3. _____ (人工供暖) hastens the growth of plants.

4. Plants can absorb carbon dioxide and _____ (释放氧气).

5. She _____ (很快就适应了) the new climate.

6. The books in the library _____ (按科目分类).

7. He started to _____ (研究生态学) and decided to devote his whole life to the science.

8. _____ (旅馆房间) was scarce during the Olympic Games.

Part IV Practical English

Notices（启事）

启事是一种公告性的通告,无论团体或个人需要向公众说明何种事情,有何种要求,需要何种帮助,即以启事的形式告知。一般采用张贴的形式,如有必要,也可登报。

启事可用于单位、团体、会议、学校、工厂等发布公告,个人也可采用以传达信息或寻求帮助。启事由标题、正文、署名和日期构成。

如：

> A Briefcase Found
>
> Dec. 12, 2005
>
> A briefcase was found, inside of which are money and other things. Owner is expected to come to identify it. Please apply at the lost property office. Open from 8:00 to 11:00 a.m. and 2:30 p.m. to 5:30 p.m.

> 公文包招领
>
> 拾到公文包一个,内有现金及其他物品。遗失者请于每日上午8:00—11:00或下午2:30—5:30,到失物招领处认领。
>
> 2005. 12. 12

Exercises

I. Fill in the blanks in the following English notice so that it is functionally equivalent to the Chinese version.

寻　人

　　长安船务公司出纳员赵华小姐，自6月1日起失踪，由该日起既未回家，也未到公司上班。任何知其行踪或有可能查明其踪迹的消息，请通知任何派出所或其家人，其地址如下：

成都中原大厦八楼803号
周同先生

Missing

　　Miss Zhao Hua, _____ of Chan'an Shipping Co., has been missing _____. She has _____ to her family nor _____ since the date mentioned. Anyone knowing the whereabouts of Miss Zhao Hua, or _____ which may lead to her location, is requested _____ any police station or _____ at the following address:

Mr. Zhou Tong
Room No. 803, 8th Floor
Zhongyuan Mansion, Chengdu

II. Write a notice with the information below.

遗　失

本人不慎将钱包遗失。如有发现者，请告知。
联系电话：13108556377

外语系王冰
2005. 11. 24

Part V English Salon

Puzzles

1. Why does the fox become a bigger animal when its head is cut off?
2. How many sides does a pail have?
3. Which letter can stand for a vegetable?
4. What thing is that you own, but often used by others?
5. I have many forests, but there are no trees in them; I have lots of rivers, but there is no water in them; I have plenty of houses, but there are no people live there. Can you guess who I am?

Try to guess the answers of the puzzles.

Vocabulary

符号说明：达到《高职高专教育英语课程教学基本要求》B级应掌握的词汇：★
　　　　达到《高职高专教育英语课程教学基本要求》A级应掌握的词汇：▲
　　　　大学英语4~6级词汇：♨

A

▲	access	/'ækses/	n.	means or right of using, reaching, or obtaining entering 取得[接近]的方法[权利]等	Unit 5
♨	accessible	/ək'sesəbl/	adj.	capable of being reached 可进入的	Unit 7
▲	adopt	/ə'dɔpt/	v.	take sb into one's family as one's child 收养	Unit 3
▲	agent	/'eidʒənt/	n.	person who acts for other people in business, politics 代理人, 经纪人	Unit 3
▲	analyze	/'ænəlaiz/	v.	look into something deeply and thoroughly 分析	Unit 1
▲	ancestor	/'ænsestə/	n.	a person in your family who lived a long time before you, from whom you are descended 祖先, 祖宗	Unit 4
★	apply	/ə'plai/	v.	put to or adapt for a special use 应用; 把……应用于	Unit 1

▲	assist	/ə'sɪst/	v.	help
				帮助，协助　Unit 3
▲	athlete	/'æθliːt/	n.	those competing in sports competitions
				运动员，运动选手　Unit 6

C

▲	collective	/kə'lektɪv/	n.	集体　Unit 7
★	competition	/ˌkɔmpɪ'tɪʃən/	n.	contest
				竞赛　Unit 2
▲	conference	/'kɔnfərəns/	n.	a meeting for consultatio
				会议，讨论会，协商会　Unit 5
★	consult	/kən'sʌlt/	v.	go to (a book, etc.) for information
				查阅[书籍等]，向[专业人士]咨询，请教　Unit 5
♨	conviction	/kən'vɪkʃən/	n.	a fixed or strong belief
				信条，信念　Unit 4
♨	cooperation	/kəuˌɔpə'reɪʃən/	n.	acting or working together for a common purpose
				合作，协作　Unit 6
★	core	/kɔː/	n.	the central or innermost part
				中心，核心　Unit 8
★	create	/krɪ'eɪt/	v.	cause to exist; bring into being
				创造，创作　Unit 2
♨	cubic	/'kjuːbɪk/	adj.	having three dimensions
				立方的　Unit 7
♨	culmination	/ˌkʌlmɪ'neɪʃən/	n.	the highest point or end of sth, usually happening after a long time
				顶点，高潮　Unit 3
★	current	/'kʌrənt/	adj.	belonging to the present time
				当前的，现在的，最近的　Unit 2

D

▲ debate	/dɪˈbeɪt/	n.	a discussion involving opposing points; an argument 辩论，争辩	Unit 1
▲ derive	/dɪˈraɪv/	v.	come from; have as an origin 得自，起源	Unit 5
▲ despair	/dɪsˈpɛə/	n.	state of having lost all hope 绝望	Unit 3
▲ digital	/ˈdɪdʒɪtl/	adj.	数字的	Unit 5
▲ discount	/ˈdɪskaʊnt/	n.	a reduction from the full amount of a price 折扣	Unit 1
▲ disk	/dɪsk/	n.	磁盘	Unit 5
♨ diversity	/daɪˈvɜːsɪti/	n.	variety 差异，多样性	Unit 7
★ document	/ˈdɔkjumənt]/	v.	support with evidence 证明	Unit 8

E

▲ electronic	/ɪlekˈtrɔnɪk/	adj.	of, or concerned with electrons 电子的	Unit 5
★ emphasize	/ˈemfəsaɪz/	v.	say sth in a strong way 强调	Unit 6
♨ evangelist	/ɪˈvændʒɪlɪst/	n.	one who practices evangelism 福音传道者	Unit 4
★ event	/ɪˈvent/	n.	a contest or an item in a sports programme 比赛项目	Unit 6
★ evidence	/ˈevɪdəns/	n.	proof 证明，证实；证据，迹象	Unit 8

171

▲ evolution	/ˌiːvəˈluːʃən, ˌevə-/	n.	the development of living things over many years from simple early forms 进化	Unit 4
♨ evolve	/iˈvɔlv/	v.	develop gradually 进化；发展	Unit 4

F

★ facility	/fəˈsiliti/	n.	设施，设备	Unit 5
♨ fantastic	/fænˈtæstik/	adj.	wonderful or superb; remarkable 美好的，极妙的	Unit 1
▲ financial	/faiˈnænʃəl/	adj.	of, or relating to finance or finances 财政的，金融的	Unit 5
♨ flexible	/ˈfleksəbl/	adj.	adaptable 可变通的；易适应的	Unit 1
▲ formula	/ˈfɔːmjulə/	n.	(US) artificial powdered milk for babies 人造婴儿奶粉	Unit 3
♨ fossil	/ˈfɔsl/	n.	the remains, on a mark, of a prehistoric animal or plant that has been buried in rock for a very long time and that has become hard 化石	Unit 8

G

★ global	/ˈgləubəl/	adj.	including the whole world 全球的，全世界的	Unit 6

H

♨ habitat	/ˈhæbitæt/	n.	environment in which an organism or

			group normally lives or occurs (动植物的)生活环境,产地,栖息地	Unit 7
♨ hectare	/ˈhektɑː/	n.	a unit of surface area equal to 10,000 square meters 公顷	Unit 7
♨ hug	/hʌɡ/	n.	strong clasp with the arms 紧紧的拥抱	Unit 3
♨ hysterics	/hiˈsteriks/	n.	wild uncontrollable emotion 歇斯底里	Unit 3

I

♨ idyllic	/aiˈdilik/	adj.	charmingly simple and serene 田园诗的	Unit 7
♨ impact	/ˈimpækt/	n.	the effect or impression of one thing on another 冲击,影响	Unit 4
♨ infant	/ˈinfənt/	n.	child during the first few years of life 婴儿,幼儿	Unit 3
★ international	/ˌintə(ː)ˈnæʃənəl/	adj.	global 国际的,世界的	Unit 2
★ interview	/ˈintəvjuː/	n.	a formal meeting in person 接见,会见	Unit 2
★ introduce	/ˌintrəˈdjuːs/	v.	bring in and establish in a new place or environment 引进,传入	Unit 6
★ involve	/inˈvɔlv/	v.	engage as a participant 卷入;使参与	Unit 1

J

| ★ journal | /'dʒɜːnl/ | n. | 报纸,定期刊物(尤其涉及某一学科) | Unit 5 |

L

| layover | /'leɪəʊvə/ | n. | (US) short stop on a journey 旅途中的短期停留 | Unit 3 |

M

▲ magnificent	/mæɡ'nɪfɪsənt/	adj.	splendid; grand 壮观的,宏伟的	Unit 8
marine	/mə'riːn/	adj.	of or relating to the sea 海的,海生的	Unit 7
meadow	/'medəʊ/	n.	grassland 草地,牧场	Unit 8
mechanism	/'mekənɪzəm/	n.	the way that sth works 机制;机构	Unit 4

O

★ occur	/ə'kɜː/	v.	take place; come about 发生;出现	Unit 4
offshore	/'ɔːfʃɔː/	adv.	away from land 离岸地	Unit 7
★ oppose	/ə'pəʊz/	v.	disagree with sth 反对,抗争	Unit 4
orbit	/'ɔːbɪt/	n.	the (usually elliptical) path described by one celestial body in its revolution about another

174

				轨道	Unit 7

♨	parade	/pəˈreid/	n.	a public procession to celebrate sth	
				游行，列队行进	Unit 6
★	perfect	/ˈpəːfikt/	adj.	excellent	
				完美的，理想的	Unit 2
♨	petrify	/ˈpetriˌfai/	v.	convert into a stony replica by petrifaction	
				石化	Unit 8
★	phenomenon	/fiˈnɔminən/	n.	sth that happens or exists	
				现象	Unit 8
★	predict	/priˈdikt/	v.	make a prediction about; tell in advance	
				预知，预言，预报	Unit 5
♨	present	/priˈzent/	v.	show or display	
				介绍；给；上演；呈现	Unit 2
▲	preserve	/priˈzəːv/	v.	maintain in safety from injury; protect	
				保护	Unit 8
★	principle	/ˈprinsəpl/	n.	a basic truth, law, or assumption	
				原则	Unit 4
♨	prominent	/ˈprɔminənt/	a.	easily seen; distinguished	
				显著的，杰出的	Unit 3
▲	prompt	/prɔmpt/	v.	help by suggesting how to continue	
				提示，提醒，指示	Unit 5

▲	range	/reindʒ/	n.	the limits within which something operates or exists	

175

			范围, 领域	Unit 5
★ rare	/rɛə/	adj.	uncommon	
			罕见的, 稀有的	Unit 8
♨ recite	/ri'sait/	v.	say aloud from memory, esp. to an audience	
			背诵; 朗诵	Unit 6
♨ refute	/ri'fjuːt/	v.	deny	
			驳斥; 否认	Unit 4
★ region	/'riːdʒən/	n.	a large area of land	
			地区, 区域	Unit 8
▲ release	/ri'liːs/	v.	let go	
			释放	Unit 6
★ religious	/ri'lidʒəs/	adj.	connected with religion	
			信奉宗教的, 虔诚的	Unit 4
▲ remote	/ri'məut/	adj.	distant in space or time	
			偏僻的, 遥远的, 远程的	Unit 5
♨ renounce	/ri'nauns/	v.	reject; give up	
			否认; 放弃	Unit 4
▲ reveal	/ri'viːl/	vt.	make clear and visible; display	
			显示, 透露	Unit 7

S

♨ scatter	/'skætə/	v.	strew or distribute over an area	
			散开, 散播	Unit 7
▲ scenery	/'siːnəri/	n.	a view or views of natural features	
			风景	Unit 8
♨ scope	/skəup/	n.	(for) space or chance for action or thought	
			余地; 机会	Unit 1
▲ selection	/si'lekʃən/	n.	act of selecting	
			选择, 挑选	Unit 4

★ sign	/sain/	n.	mark, symbol, etc. used to represent sth 标记, 符号; 征兆, 迹象; 标牌, 招牌	Unit 2
sparkle	/'spɑːkl/	n.	a glittering quality 闪亮; 闪光的性质	Unit 1
▲ specialize	/'speʃəlaiz/	v.	make specific mention of; particularize 特指……; 限定	Unit 1
species	/'spiːʃiz/	n.	a group of plants or animals that are similar to each other 种类	Unit 4
spiritual	/'spiritjuəl/	a.	of the human spirit 精神的, 心灵的	Unit 3
★ spot	/spɔt/	v.	detect or discern, especially visually 辨认, 认出	Unit 8
spray	/sprei/	v.	scatter in the form of tiny particles 喷射, 喷溅	Unit 8
stadium	/'steidiəm/	n.	a large, usually open structure for sports events 体育场, 运动场	Unit 6
▲ status	/'steitəs/	n.	position relative to that of others 地位, 身份	Unit 6
subsequently	/'sʌbsikwəntli/	ad.	after an event in the past 后来, 随后	Unit 4
survival	/sə'vaivəl/	n.	the state of continuing to live or exist 生存, 幸存	Unit 4
▲ sweater	/'swetə/	n.	close-fitting knitted garment without fastening 针织紧身套衫	Unit 3

symbolize	/ˈsimbəlaiz/	v.	serve as a symbol of 象征	Unit 6

T

theme	/θi:m/	n.	main subject or idea 主题，题目	Unit 6
traditional	/trəˈdiʃ(ə)l/	adj.	of, relating to, or in accord with tradition 传统的，惯例的	Unit 6
tremendous	/triˈmendəs/	adj.	enormous 强烈地；极大的	Unit 4
tropical	/ˈtrɔpikl/	adj.	of or relating to the tropics 热带的	Unit 7

V

variation	/ˌvɛəriˈeiʃən/	n.	a difference in quality or quantity befween a lot of things 进化，变异	Unit 4
version	/ˈvə:ʃən/	n.	a form of a written or musical work 版本	Unit 5
vessel	/ˈvesl/	n.	a ship or large boat 船；舰	Unit 7

W

web	/web/	n.	a net of thin threads 网	Unit 5
wolf	/wulf/	n.	a wide animal that looks like a dog and that lives and hunts in a group 狼	Unit 8